NATIONAL ANTHEMS
OF THE WORLD

NATIONAL ANTHEMS OF THE WORLD

ELEVENTH EDITION

Edited by

Michael Jamieson Bristow

WEIDENFELD & NICOLSON

First published in Great Britain in 1960
Second Edition 1963
Third Edition 1969
Fourth Edition 1975
Fifth Edition 1978
Sixth Edition 1985
Seventh Edition 1987
Eighth Edition 1993
Ninth Edition 1997
Reprinted 1998
Tenth Edition 2002
Eleventh Edition 2006

1 3 5 7 9 10 8 6 4 2

© Weidenfeld & Nicolson 1960, 1963, 1969, 1975, 1978, 1985, 1987, 1993, 1997, 2002 and 2006

Distributed in the United States by
Sterling Publishing Co., Inc.,
387 Park Avenue South, New York, N.Y. 10016-8810

A CIP catalogue record for this book is available from the British Library.

ISBN-13   9 780304 368266
ISBN-10   0 304 36826 1

Music and text set by Lancaster Music Setting, Huddersfield
Printed in Great Britain by The Bath Press, Bath

Weidenfeld & Nicolson
The Orion Publishing Group Ltd
Orion House
5 Upper Saint Martin's Lane
London, WC2H 9EA
www.orionbooks.co.uk

The Orion Publishing Group's policy is to use papers that are natural, renewable and recyclable products and made from wood grown in sustainable forests. The logging and manufacturing processes are expected to conform to the environmental regulations of the country of origin.

CONTENTS

Preface 7

A

Afghanistan . . . 9
Albania 12
Algeria 14
Andorra 18
Angola 22
Antigua and Barbuda 26
Argentina . . . 28
Armenia 36
Australia 38
Austria 40
Azerbaijan . . . 42

B

Bahamas, The . . 46
Bahrain 49
Bangladesh . . . 51
Barbados 56
Belarus 59
Belgium 62
Belize 66
Bénin 70
Bhutan 74
Bolivia 77
Bosnia and Herzegovina 82
Botswana 84
Brazil 86
Brunei Darussalam . 94
Bulgaria 96
Burkina Faso . . . 98
Burundi 102

C

Cambodia . . . 107
Cameroon . . . 110
Canada 114
Cape Verde . . . 117
Central African Republic 121
Chad 124
Chile 127
China 135
Colombia 138
Comoros, The . . 142
Congo
(Democratic Republic) 146
Congo (Republic) . 150
Costa Rica . . . 154

Croatia . . . 159
Cuba 161
Cyprus 164
Czech Republic . . 167

D

Denmark 169
Djibouti 172
Dominica 174
Dominican Republic . 176

E

Ecuador 180
Egypt 186
El Salvador . . . 189
Equatorial Guinea . 199
Eritrea 203
Estonia 206
Ethiopia 208

F

Fiji 211
Finland 214
France 216

G

Gabon 219
Gambia, The . . . 223
Georgia 225
Germany 227
Ghana 229
Gibraltar 232
Greece 235
Grenada 238
Guatemala . . . 240
Guinea 244
Guinea-Bissau . . 246
Guyana 250

H

Haiti 252
Honduras 256
Hungary 261

I

Iceland 264
India 267
Indonesia 272
Iran 277
Iraq 279

Irish Republic . . 280
Isle of Man . . . 282
Israel 284
Italy 286
Ivory Coast . . . 290

J

Jamaica 293
Japan 295
Jordan 296

K

Kazakhstan . . . 297
Kenya 300
Kiribati 302
Korea (North) . . 304
Korea (South) . . 307
Kuwait 309
Kyrgyzstan . . . 313

L

Laos 316
Latvia 319
Lebanon 321
Lesotho 324
Liberia 326
Libya 329
Liechtenstein . . 333
Lithuania 335
Luxembourg . . 337

M

Macedonia . . . 340
Madagascar . . . 342
Malawi 345
Malaysia 348
Maldives, The . . 350
Mali 352
Malta 356
Marshall Islands . . 358
Mauritania . . . 361
Mauritius 365
Mexico 367
Micronesia . . . 372
Moldova 373
Monaco 376
Mongolia 379
Morocco 382
Mozambique . . . 385
Myanmar 388

N

Namibia	390
Nauru	392
Nepal	395
Netherlands	397
New Zealand	399
Nicaragua	401
Niger	404
Nigeria	409
Norway	411

O

Oman	414

P

Pakistan	417
Palau	420
Panama	422
Papua New Guinea	426
Paraguay	428
Peru	435
Philippines, The	440
Poland	445
Portugal	447

Q

Qatar	451

R

Romania	454
Russian Federation	458
Rwanda	461

S

Saint Kitts and Nevis	467
Saint Lucia	469
Saint Vincent and The Grenadines	471
Samoa	473
San Marino	476
São Tomé and Prncipe	478
Saudi Arabia	481
Scotland	483
Sénégal	489
Serbia and Montenegro	494
Seychelles	496
Sierra Leone	499
Singapore	501
Slovakia	503
Slovenia	505
Solomon Islands	507
Somalia	509
South Africa	510

Spain	514
Sri Lanka	517
Sudan	521
Surinam	524
Swaziland	526
Sweden	529
Switzerland	531
Syria	536

T

Taiwan	539
Tajikistan	541
Tanzania	544
Thailand	546
Timor-Leste	548
Togo	551
Tonga	554
Trinidad and Tobago	556
Tunisia	558
Turkey	560
Turkmenistan	563
Tuvalu	566

U

Uganda	569
Ukraine	570
United Arab Emirates	573
United Kingdom	576
United States of America	578
Uruguay	581
Uzbekistan	590

V

Vanuatu	593
Vatican City State	596
Venezuela	603
Vietnam	607

W

Wales	610

Y

Yemen	613

Z

Zambia	616
Zimbabwe	619

European Union	622

National Days	624

PREFACE

National Anthems of the World was originally published in 1960 and this Eleventh Edition includes substantial changes to the world's National Anthems.

Replacement National Anthems are included for Bosnia and Herzegovina, Georgia, Mozambique, Rwanda and Somalia whilst there are new words for the National Anthems of Antigua & Barbuda, Belarus and Ukraine. It has been possible in this Edition to now include words for Mauritania, Qatar, San Marino (unofficial), Tajikistan, Turkmenistan and the United Arab Emirates and to add the German words for Belgium, the Creole words for Haiti and the Latin words for the Vatican City State, whilst a replacement vocal text for Syria has been revised. Monaco has a longer version. New arrangements have also been added for Armenia, Bhutan, Brunei Darussalam, Congo (Democratic Republic), Denmark, Dominica, Ghana, India, Micronesia, Oman, Papua New Guinea, Romania, Solomon Islands, Tuvalu, Vanuatu and Zambia. The only nation to have gained recent independence has been Timor-Leste and their new National Anthem is included in this Edition along with Scotland.

There are examples of some National Anthems where, regrettably, it has not been possible to fit the words to the music, as no vocal scores have been supplied to the editor.

The list of National Days has been revised and updated.

Where a National Anthem is in a language that is not written in the Roman script, the words are given in a transliterated phonetic version.

The editor would like to express his thanks for the valuable help and advice given to him by Reinhard Popp in Germany; to Fabio Lazzati in Italy; to Joachim Kolb in London; to the publishers Philipp Reclam Jun., in Stuttgart and to the various Embassies and High Commissions, who have supplied valuable information concerning their National Anthems.

Effort has been made to trace copyright ownership, and it is regretted if any acknowledgments have been unwittingly omitted. In most cases the version of the melody and the accompaniment is that officially authorised by the State. Where piano arrangements and translations have been specially made, these may not be reproduced without the permission of The Orion Publishing Group Limited.

It is hoped that this Eleventh Edition will be a useful reference book, not only for the number of occasions on which it is required to sing or play a particular National Anthem, but also as a record of the aspirations of the whole family of nations.

M.J.B.

May 2006

AFGHANISTAN

Author unknown

Music by
USTAD QASIM (1887 - 1957)
Arr. by VOLKER WÖRRLEIN

This National Anthem was adopted in 1992, abolished in 1999 and restored in 2002.
It is to be replaced in the near future.

Sorud-e melli-ye Afghanistan
Qal'a-ye Islam, qalb-e Asiya,
Jawidan azad khak-e Ariya,
Zadgah-e qahramanan-e bozorg,
Sangar-e razmande-ye mardan-e khoda
Allahu akbar, Allahu akbar, Allahu akbar.

Tigh-e imanash be meydan-e jihad,
Band-e estebdad-ra az ham gozast
Mellat-e azade Afghanistan
Dar jehan zanjir-e mahkuman shekest.
Allahu akbar, Allahu akbar, Allahu akbar.

Sar-e khatt-e qur'an nizam-e ma bowad,
Parcham-e iman be bam-e ma bowad,
Ham seda o-ham nawa ba ham rawan,
Wahdat-emelli muram-e ma bowad.
Allahu akbar, Allahu akbar, Allahu akbar.

Shad zey, azad zey, abad zey,
Ey watan dar nur-e qanun-e khoda.
Mash'al-e azadegi-ra bar firaz,
Mardom-e sar-goshte-ra shou rahnama.
Allahu akbar, Allahu akbar, Allahu akbar.

Translation by Joachim Kolb

Fortress of Islam, heart of Asia,
Forever free, soil of the Aryans,
Birthplace of great heroes,
Fellow traveller of the warriors of the men of God,
God is great! God is great! God is great!

Arrow of His faith to the arena of Jihad,
Removing the shackles of suppression,
The nation of freedom, Afghanistan,
Breaks the chains of the oppressed in the world.
God is great! God is great! God is great!

Let the lines of the Koran be our order,
Let the banner of faith be on our roof,
With the echoes and the voices going together,
Let national unity be what we strive for,
God is great! God is great! God is great!

Live happy, live free, live and prosper,
Oh homeland in the light of God's law,
Lift the torch of freedom high,
Become a leader for the people who are oppressed,
God is great! God is great! God is great!

ALBANIA
Hymni i Flamurit
(Hymn to the Flag)

Words by
ALEKSANDER STAVRE DRENOVA (1872 - 1947)

Music by
CIPRIAN PORUMBESCU (1853 - 1883)
Arr. by HENRY COLEMAN

Music composed in 1880. Adopted in 1912.

luf - te veç a - y lar - go - het Që ë - shtë lin - dur tra - dhë -

tor, Kush ë - shtë bu - rrë nuk fri - ko - het Po

vdes, po vdes si një dë - shmor. Prej - shmor.

cresc. molto

ff

pp

Translation

The flag which in battle unites us
Found us all ready for the oath,
One mind, one aim, until our land
Becomes free from the enemy.

CHORUS

We stand in the battle for right and freedom,
The enemies of the people stand alone,
The hero dedicates his life to our land,
Even in dying he will be brave.

ALGERIA

Words by
MUFDI ZAKARIAH (1930-1978)

Music by
MOHAMED FAWZI (1918-1966)
Arr. by TAREK HASSAN

1. Qa-ssa - man Bin-na - zi - la-t Il-ma-hi-qat_____ Wad - di-

maa Iz - za - ki - ya-t It-ta - hi - rat._____ Qa-ssa -

Adopted in 1963.

2. *Nah-no Gon-don Fi Sa-bi-l_Il hakki Thor-na*
   Wa I-la Iss-tiq-la-li-na Bil-har-bi Kum-na.
   Lam Ya-kon Yoss-gha La-na Lam-ma Na-tak-na
   Fat-ta-khath-na Ran-na-t_Al-ba-roo-di Waz-na.
   Wa Azaf-na Na-gha-ma-t_Al-rash-sha-shi Lah-na
   Wa A-qad-na_Al-azma An Tah-ya_Al-ga-za-ir.
      Fash-ha-doo! Fash-ha-doo! Fash-ha-doo!

3. *Nah-no min Ab-ta-li-na Nad-fa-oo Gon-dan*
   Wa A-la Ash-la-ina Nass-na-oo Mag-dan.
   Wa A-la Ar-wa-he-na Nass-a-do Khul-dan
   Wa A-la Ha-ma-ti-na Nar-fa-o Ban-dan.
   Gab-ha-to 'L-tah-ree-ri Aa-tay-na-ki Ah-dan
   Wa A-qad-na_Al-azma An Tah-ya_Al-ga-za-ir.
      Fash-ha-doo! Fash-ha-doo! Fash-ha-doo!

4. *Sar-kha-to `l-aw-ta-ni min Sa-h_Il-fi-da*
   Iss-ma-oo-ha Wass-ta-gee-bo Lin-ni-da
   Wak-to-boo-ha Bi-di-maa Il-sho-ha-daa
   Wak-ra-oo-ha Li-ba-ny_Il-geeli gha-dan.
   Kad Ma-dad-na La-ka Ya Mag-do Ya-da
   Wa A-qad-na Al-azma An Tah-ya_Al-ga-za-ir.
      Fash-ha-doo! Fash-ha-doo! Fash-ha-doo!

French Translation

1. *Par les foudres qui anéantissent,*
   Par les flots de sang pur et sans tache,
   Par les drapeaux flottants qui flottent
   Sur les hauts djebels orgueilleux et fiers,
   Nous jurons nous être révoltés pour vivre ou pour mourir,
   Et nous avons juré de mourir pour que vive l 'Algérie!
      Témoignez! Témoignez! Témoignez!

2. *Nous sommes des soldats pour la justice, révoltés,*
   Et pour notre indépendance nous avons engagé le combat,
   Nous n'avons obéi à nulle injonction en nous soulevant.
   Le bruit de la poudre a été notre mesure
   Et le crépitement des mitrailleuses notre chant favori.
   Et nous avons juré de mourir pour que vive l 'Algérie!
      Témoignez! Témoignez! Témoignez!

3. *Sur nos héros nous bâtirons une gloire*
   Et sur nos corps nous monterons à l 'immortalité,
   Sur nos âmes, nous construirons une armée
   Et de notre espoir nous lèverons l'étendard.
   Front de la libération, nous t'avons prêté serment
   Et nous avons juré de mourir pour que vive l'Algérie!
      Témoignez! Témoignez! Témoignez!

4. *Le cri de la patrie monte des champs de bataille.*
   Ecoutez-le et répondez à l'appel.
   Ecrivez-le dans le sang des martyrs
   Et dictez-le aux générations futures.
   Nous t'avons donné la main, ô gloire,
   Et nous avons juré de mourir pour que vive I 'Algérie!
      Témoignez! Témoignez! Témoignez!

Translation by T. M. Cartledge
(from the French)

1. We swear by the lightning that destroys,
   By the streams of generous blood being shed,
   By the bright flags that wave,
   Flying proudly on the high djebels,
   That we are in revolt, whether to live or to die,
   We are determined that Algeria should live,
   So be our witness - be our witness - be our witness!

2. We are soldiers in revolt for truth
   And we have fought for our independence.
   When we spoke, nobody listened to us,
   So we have taken the noise of gunpowder as our rhythm
   And the sound of machine-guns as our melody,
   We are determined that Algeria should live,
   So be our witness - be our witness - be our witness!

3. From our heroes we shall make an army come to being,
   From our dead we shall build up a glory,
   Our spirits shall ascend to immortality
   And on our shoulders we shall raise the Standard.
   To the nation's Liberation Front we have sworn an oath,
   We are determined that Algeria should live,
   So be our witness - be our witness - be our witness!

4. The cry of the Fatherland sounds from the battlefields.
   Listen to it and answer the call!
   Let it be written with the blood of martyrs
   And be read to future generations.
   Oh, Glory, we have held out our hand to you,
   We are determined that Algeria should live,
   So be our witness - be our witness - be our witness!

ANDORRA

Words by
JOAN BENLLOCH I VIVÓ (1864-1926)

Music by
ENRIC MARFANY BONS (1871-1942)

El gran Car - le - many, mon Pa - re, dels a - larbs em des - lliu - rà, _____ I del cel vi - da em do - nà _____ de Me - rit - xell, la gran Ma - re, Prin - ce - sa nasquí i Pu -

Became officially the National Anthem on 8 September, 1914, the anniversary day of the Jungfrau von Meritxell, patron saint of Andorra.

bi - lla en - tre dues na - cions neu - tral_____ Sols

res - to l'ú - ni - ca fi - lla de l'im - pe - ri Car - le -

many. Cre - ient i lliu - re on - ze se - gles, cre -

ient i lliu - re vull ser.   ¡Si - guin els furs mos tu -

tors i mos Prín - ceps de - fen - sors! i mos Prin - ceps de - fen -

sors!

20

Translation

The great Charlemagne, my Father, liberated me from the Saracens,
And from heaven he gave me life of Meritxell the great Mother.
I was born a Princess, a Maiden neutral between two nations;
I am the only remaining daughter of the Carolingian empire.
Believing and free for eleven centuries, believing and free I will be.
The laws of the land be my tutors, and Princes my defender!
And Princes my defender!

ANGOLA

Words by
MANUEL RUI ALVES MONTEIRO (*b.* 1941)

Music by
RUI ALBERTO VIEIRA DIAS MINGAO (*b.* 1939)
Arr. by W. L. REED

Martially

1. O Pá - tria, nun - ca mais es - que - ce - re - mos os he -
róis do qua - tro de Fe - ve - rei - o. O
Pá - tria, nós sau - da - mos os teus fi - lhos tom -

Adopted in 1975.
New replacement words are expected in the future.

ção, pe - lo Po - der Po - pu - lar! Pá - tria U -

ni - da, Li - ber - da - de, um só Po - vo, u - ma só Na - ção!

28

31

2. *Levantemos nossas vozes libertadas*
   Para glória dos povos africanos.
   Marchemos, combatentes angolanos,
   Solidários com os povos oprimidos.
   Orgulhosos lutaremos pela Paz
   Com as forças progressistas do mundo.
   Orgulhosos lutaremos pela Paz
   Com as forças progressistas do mundo.

   CHORUS
   Angola, avante!
   Revolução, pelo Poder Popular!
   Pátria Unida, Liberdade,
   Um só Povo, uma só Nação!   } (twice)

Translation

1. O Fatherland, we shall never forget
   The heroes of the Fourth of February.
   O Fatherland, we salute your sons
   Who died for our independence.
   We honour the past and our history
   As by our work we build the New Man.

   CHORUS
   Forward, Angola!
   Revolution through the power of the People! } (twice)
   A United Country, Freedom,
   One People, one Nation!

2. Let us raise our liberated voices
   To the glory of the peoples of Africa.
   We shall march, Angolan fighters,
   In solidarity with oppressed peoples.
   We shall fight proudly for Peace
   Along with the progressive forces of the world.

   CHORUS

25

ANTIGUA AND BARBUDA

Words by
NOVELLE HAMILTON RICHARDS (1917 - 1986)

Music by
WALTER GARNET PICART CHAMBERS (1908 - 2003)

1. Fair An - ti - gua and Bar - bu - da We thy sons and daugh - ters stand, Strong and firm in peace or dan - ger. To safe - guard our Na - tive land. We com - mit our -

Originally adopted in 1967 on achieving statehood. New words adopted in 1981 when achieving independence.

selves to build - ing A true na - tion brave and free.

Ev - er striv - ing, ev - er seek - ing, Dwell in love and un - i - ty.

2. Raise the standard! Raise it boldly!
   Answer now to duty's call
   To the service of thy country,
   Sparing nothing, giving all;
   Gird your loins and join the battle
   'Gainst fear, hate and poverty,
   Each endeavouring, all achieving,
   Live in peace where man is free.

3. God of nations, let Thy blessings
   Fall upon this land of ours;
   Rain and sunshine ever sending,
   Fill her fields with crops and flowers;
   We her children do implore Thee,
   Give us strength, faith, loyalty,
   Never failing, all enduring
   To defend her liberty.

ARGENTINA
Marcha de la Patria
(March of the Fatherland)

Words by
VICENTE LÓPEZ Y PLANES (1785 - 1856)

Music by
JOSÉ BLAS PARERA (1765 - 1830)
Arr. by JUAN PEDRO ESNAOLA
and LUIS N. LARETA

Officially adopted on 11 May, 1813. There are nine verses.

28

tad, li - ber - tad, li - ber - tad! O - id el

 rui - do de ro - tas ca - de - nas; Ved en

tro - no a la no - ble I - gual - dad.

¡Ya— su tro - no dig - ni - si - mo a - brie - ron Las Pro-

vin - cias U - ni - das del Sud! Y los

li - bres del mun - do res - pon - den: ¡Al gran

pue - blo Ar - gen - ti - no, Sa - lud! ¡Al gran

pue - blo Ar - gen - ti - no, Sa - lud! Y los

li - bres del mun - do res - pon - den: ¡Al gran

pue - blo_Ar - gen - ti - no, Sa - lud! Y___ los

li - bres del mun - do res - pon - den: ¡Al gran

pue - blo_Ar - gen - ti - no, Sa - lud!

Allegro vivace (♩ = 126)

CHORUS

Sean e - ter - nos los lau -

(♩ = 76)

re - les,   Que su - pi - mos con - se - guir: Que su-

Lento (♩ = 66)

pi - mos con - se - guir: Co - ro - na - dos de glo - ria vi -

lunga

Allegro vivace (♩ = 144)

va - mos O— ju - re - mos con glo - ria mo - rir. O ju -

re - mos con glo - ria mo - rir. O ju -

re - mos con glo - ria mo - rir.

73

Translation

Mortals! Hear the sacred cry;
Freedom! Freedom! Freedom!
Hear the noise of broken chains.
See noble Equality enthroned.
The United Provinces of the South
Have now displayed their worthy throne.
And the free peoples of the world reply; } (twice)
We salute the great people of Argentina !

CHORUS
May the laurels be eternal
That we knew how to win.
Let us live crowned with glory,
Or swear to die gloriously. (three times)

ARMENIA
Mer Hayrenik
(Our Fatherland)

Words adapted from a poem by
MIQAYÉL GHAZARI NALBANDYAN (1829 - 1866)

Music by
BARSEGH KANACHYAN (1885 - 1967)

Officially adopted on 1 July, 1991.

2. *Aha yeghbayr qez mi drôsh,*
   Zor im dzerqov gordsetsi.
   Gishernerd yes qoun chegha,
   Artasouqov lvatsi. } (twice)

3. *Nayir nran yereq gouynov,*
   Nvirakan mék nshan,
   T'ogh p'oghp'oghi t'shnamou dém, } (twice)
   T'ogh misht pandsa Hayastan.

4. *Amenayn tegh mahd mi é*
   Mard mi angam pit merni,
   Bayts yerani vor iur azgi } (twice)
   Azatout'yan kd zohvi.

Translation by E. V. Gulbekian

1. Land of our fathers, free, independent,
   Which has endured from age to age.
   Its sons and daughters now proclaim } (twice)
   Armenia, sovereign and free.

2. Brother, take this banner,
   Made with my own hands,
   During sleepless nights, } (twice)
   And bathed in my tears.

3. See, it has three colours;
   A single hallowed symbol.
   May it sparkle before the foe, } (twice)
   May Armenia flourish ever!

4. Death is everywhere the same,
   Man is born just once to die,
   But blest is he who gives his life } (twice)
   To defend his nation's freedom.

AUSTRALIA
Advance Australia Fair

Words and music by
PETER DODDS McCORMICK (1834 - 1916)
Arr. by W. L. REED

1. Aus - tra - lians all, let us re - joice, For we are young and free; We've gold - en soil and wealth for toil, Our home is girt by sea. Our land a - bounds in Na - ture's gifts Of beau - ty rich and rare; In

Adopted officially as the National Anthem on 19 April, 1984. The words were then slightly changed. The National Anthem of Australia is also used on Norfolk Island.

his - t'rys page let ev - 'ry stage Ad - vance Aus - tra - lia fair.

CHORUS

In joy - ful strains then let us sing, "Ad - vance Aus - tra - lia Fair."

2. Beneath our radiant Southern Cross
   We'll toil with hearts and hands;
   To make this Commonwealth of ours
   Renowned of all the lands;
   For those who've come across the seas
   We've boundless plains to share;
   With courage let us all combine
   To Advance Australia fair.

   CHORUS

AUSTRIA
Bundeshymne
(Federal Hymn)

Words by
PAULA von PRERADOVIĆ (1887 - 1951)

Music by
WOLFGANG AMADEUS MOZART (1756 - 1791) or
JOHANN HOLZER (1753 - 1818) *
Arr. by VIKTOR KELDORFER

Officially adopted on 25 February, 1947.

*Wolfgang Amadeus Mozart (1756 - 1791) has been claimed as the composer, but the evidence is more in Holzer's favour, according to Austrian scholarship.

40

Volk, be - gna - det für das — Schö - ne, Viel - ge - rühm - tes

Ö - ster - reich, Viel - ge - rühm - tes — Ö - ster - reich.

2. Heiss umfehdet, wild umstritten,
   Liegst dem Erdteil du inmitten
   Einem starken Herzen gleich.
   Hast seit Frühen Ahnentagen
   Hoher Sendung Last getragen,
   Vielgeprüftes Österreich, Vielgeprüftes Österreich.

3. Mutig in die neuen Zeiten,
   Frei und gläubig sieh uns schreiten,
   Arbeitsfroh und hoffnungsreich.
   Einig lass in Brüderchören,
   Vaterland, dir Treue schwören,
   Vielgeliebtes Österreich, Vielgeliebtes Österreich.

Translation

1. Land of mountains, land on the River*,
   Land of fields, land of spires,
   Land of hammers, with a rich future,
   You are the home of great sons,
   A nation blessed by its sense of beauty,
   Highly praised Austria, highly praised Austria.

2. Strongly fought for, fiercely contested,
   You are in the centre of the Continent
   Like a strong heart,
   You have borne since the earliest days
   The burden of a high mission,
   Much tried Austria, much tried Austria.

3. Watch us striding free and believing,
   With courage, into new eras,
   Working cheerfully and full of hope,
   In fraternal chorus let us take in unity
   The oath of allegiance to you, our country,
   Our much beloved Austria, our much beloved Austria.

* the Danube

41

AZERBAIJAN
Azerbaijan Marsi
(Azerbaijan March)

Words by
AHMED JAVAD (1892 - 1937)

Music by
UZEIR GADJIBECOV (1885 - 1948)
Arr. by W. L. REED

The words and music of the National Anthem were written in 1919. Officially adopted on 27 May, 1992.

A - zer - bai - jan!   A - zer - bai - jan!

Translation

Azerbaijan! Azerbaijan!
O Great Land, your children are heroes.
We are ready to be martyred for you.
We are ready to shed blood for you.
Three-coloured flag, flourish honourably!
Thousands of lives have been sacrificed.
Your bosom has become a battlefield.
Every devoted soldier
Has become a hero.
You are prospering.
My life is always dedicated to you.
My love for you is embedded in my heart
A thousand and one times.
To preserve everything
And to honour her flag
All the youth are willing.
Great Land! Great Land!
Azerbaijan! Azerbaijan!

THE BAHAMAS
March On, Bahamaland

Words and music by
TIMOTHY GIBSON (1903 - 1978)
Arr. by W. L. REED

Selected as a result of a competition and adopted when the country became independent on 10 July, 1973.

sun - ward, though the wea - ther hide the wide and treach - 'rous shoal. Lift up your head to the ris - ing sun, Ba - ha - ma-land; Till the road you've trod Lead un - to your God, March— on, Ba - ha - ma - land!

BAHRAIN

Words by
MOHAMED SUDQI AYYASH (1925 - 2000)

Composer unknown
Arr. by MOHAMED SUDQI AYYASH

Allegretto alla marcia

Bah - rai - no - na___ Ba - la - dol - a - man___ Wa - ta - nol ki - ram,___ Yah - mi Hi ma - ha A - mi - ru - nal Ho - mam; Qa - mat - a - la - Ha - dy - el - r - e - sa - la - te, Wal A - da - la - ti Wal Sa -

Adopted in 1971.

49

- lam! A - Shat Daw - la - tol Bah - rain___ Ba - la - dol - a - rain.

Translation

Our Bahrain,
Country of security,
Nation of hospitality,
Protected by our courageous Amir,
Founded on the principles of the Message,
Justice and Peace,
Long live the State of Bahrain!

BANGLADESH

Words and music by
RABINDRANATH TAGORE (1861 - 1941) *
Arr. by T. M. CARTLEDGE

Officially adopted in April 1971.
* Rabindranath Tagore also wrote the words and music of the National Anthem of India.

O - mã ã - mãr prã - né___ bã - ĵaý bã - śi.___ So - nãr___

Bãn - glã,___ Ã - mi to - mãý___ bhã - lo -

bã - si.___ O mã, Fã - gu - ne tor
kū - le___ Mã,___ tor mu - kher bã - nī___

ã - mer___ ba - ne___ ghrã - ne___ pã - gal ka - re,
ã - mãr___ kã - ne___ lã - ge,___ su - dhar ma - to,

D. % al Fine

D. % al Fine

ye - chā — ba - ter   mū - le,   na - dir ____ kū - le ____

91

Translation

My Bengal of gold, I love you.
Forever your skies, your air set my heart in tune
As if it were a flute.
In spring, O mother mine, the fragrance from your mango groves
Makes me wild with joy –
Ah, what a thrill!

In autumn, O mother mine,
In the full-blossomed paddy fields
I have seen spread all over – sweet smiles.
Ah, what a beauty, what shades, what an affection
And what a tenderness!
What a quilt have you spread at the feet of banyan trees
And along the banks of rivers!

O mother mine, words from your lips
Are like nectar to my ears.
Ah, what a thrill!
If sadness, O mother mine, casts a gloom on your face,
My eyes are filled with tears!

BARBADOS

Words by
IRVING LOUIS BURGIE (*b.* 1926)

Music by
ROLAND EDWARDS (1912 - 1985)
Arr. by W. L. REED

1. In— plen-ty and in time of need When this fair land was young. Our— brave fore-fa-thers sowed the seed From which our pride is sprung, A pride that makes no wan-ton boast Of what it has with -

Adopted on 30 November, 1966.

stood, That binds our hearts from coast to coast – The pride of na - tion -

ff **CHORUS**

hood. We loy - al sons and daugh - ters all Do

here - by make it known These fields and hills be -

yond re - call Are now our ve - ry own. We write our names on

2. The Lord has been the people's guide
   For past three hundred years.
   With Him still on the people's side
   We have no doubts or fears.
   Upward and onward we shall go,
   Inspired, exulting, free,
   And greater will our nation grow
   In strength and unity.

   CHORUS

BELARUS

Words by
MIKHAS KLIMKOVICH (1899 - 1954)
and ULADZIMIER KARYZNA (*b.* 1938)

Music by
NESTER SAKALOUSKI (1902 - 1950)

Adopted on 24 September, 1955.
New revised words adopted in 2002.

1. *My, bjelarusy - mirnyja l'judzi,*
   Sercam addanyja rodnaj zjaml'l,
   Shchyra sjabrujem, sily hartujem
   My ŭ pracavitaj, vol'naj sjam'ji.

   CHORUS
   Slaŭsja, zjaml'l nashaj svjetlaje imja,
   Slausja, narodaŭ braterski sajuz!
   Nasha l'jubimaja maci -Radzima,
   Vjechna zhyvi i kvitnjej, Bjelarusj!

2. *Razam z bratami muzhna vjakami*
   My baranili rodny paroh,
   U bitvakh za vol'ju, bitvakh za dol'ju
   Svoj zdabyvali scjab pjeramoh!

   CHORUS

3. *Druzhba narodaŭ - sila narodaŭ -*
   Nash zapavjetny, sonjechny shljakh.
   Horda zh uzvisja ŭ jasnyja wysi,
   Scjah pjeramozhny - radasci scjah!

   CHORUS

Translation

1. We, the Belarusians, peaceful people,
   Our heart is to our native land,
   We maintain generous friendship and gain our powers
   Within the industrious, free family.

   CHORUS
   Glory to the bright name of our land,
   Glory to the fraternal union of our peoples!
   Our beloved mother-Motherland,
   Long you live and flourish, Belarus!

2. Together with brothers, with fortitude, during centuries
   We guarded our native thresholds,
   In struggles for freedom, in struggles for fate,
   We have been gaining our banner of victories.

   CHORUS

3. The friendship of peoples (which is) the power of peoples
   Is our venerable, sunny path
   You soar up proudly, into the bright heights,
   The banner of victory, the banner of joy.

   CHORUS

BELGIUM

La Brabançonne
(The Song of Brabant)

French words by
CHARLES LATOUR ROGIER (1800 - 1885)

Dutch words by
VICTOR CEULEMANS (1887 - 1969)

Music by
FRANÇOIS van CAMPENHOUT (1779 - 1848)

Adopted in 1830.

Official version of the Dutch words written in 1918 were officially adopted in 1938.

Roi, la Loi, la Li - ber - té,
Vorst, voor vrij - heid en voor recht,

Au -
Het woord ge -

ra pour___ de - vise im - mor - tel - le:
trouw dat ge on be - vreesd moogt spre - ken:

Le
Voor

Roi, la Loi, la Li - ber - té,
Vorst, voor vrij - heid en voor recht,

Le
Voor

Roi, la Loi, la Li - ber - té,
Vorst, voor vrij - heid en voor recht,

Le
Voor

poco allarg.

poco allarg.

Roi, la Loi, la Li - ber - té.
Voorst, voor vrij - heid en voor recht.

German version

O liebes Land, O Belgiens Erde,
Dir unser Herz, Dir unsere Hand,
Dir unser Blut, dem Heimatherde,
Wir schwören's Dir, O Vaterland!
So blühe froh in voller Schöne,
Zu der die Freiheit Dich erzog,
Und fortan singen Deine Söhne:
Gesetz und König und die Feiheit hoch! } (three times)

Translation of the French version by W. L. Reed

Noble Belgium - for ever a dear land -
We give you our hearts and our arms.
By the pure blood spilt for you, our Fatherland,
We swear with one cry - You will live!
You will live, always great and beautiful,
And your invincible unity
Will have as your immortal emblem -
For King, Justice and Liberty! } (three times)

Translation of the Flemish version by T. M. Cartledge

O beloved Belgium, sacred land of our fathers,
Our heart and soul are dedicated to you.
Our strength and the blood of our veins we offer,
Be our goal, in work and battle.
Prosper, O country, in unbreakable unity,
Always be yourself and free.
Trust in the word that, undaunted, you can speak:
For King, for Freedom and for Law. } (three times)

BELIZE

Words by
SAMUEL ALFRED HAYNES (1898 - 1971)

Music by
SELWYN WALFORD YOUNG (1899 - 1977)
Arr. by W. L. REED

1. O Land of the Free by the Ca - rib Sea, Our man - hood we pledge to thy li - ber - ty! No ty - rants here lin - ger, des - pots must flee This tran - quil ha - ven of de - mo - cra - cy. The

Officially adopted upon independence on 21 September, 1981.

blood of our sires, which hal - lows the sod, Brought

free - dom from slav - 'ry, op - pres - sion's rod, By the

might of truth and the grace of God. No

CHORUS

lon - ger shall___ we be hew - ers of wood. A -

Land of the Free by the Ca - rib Sea!

2. Nature has blessed thee with wealth untold,
   O'er mountains and valleys where prairies roll;
   Our fathers, the Baymen, valiant and bold
   Drove back th'invader, this heritage bold
   From proud Rio Hondo to old Sarstoon,
   Through coral isle, over blue lagoon,
   Keep watch with the angels, the stars and moon.
   For freedom comes tomorrow's noon.

   CHORUS

BÉNIN

L'Aube Nouvelle
(The Dawn of a New Day)

Words and music by
GILBERT JEAN DAGNON (*b.* 1926)
Arr. by HENRY COLEMAN

Con spirito

1. Ja - dis à son ap - pel, nos aï -
eux sans fai - bles - se Ont su a -
vec cou - rage, ar - deur, pleins d'al - lé - gres - se Li -

Adopted on 30 July, 1960.
The chorus is usually sung on its own.

70

vrer au prix du sang des com - bats é - cla - tants. Ac - cou-

rez vous aus-si, bâ - tis - seurs du pré - sent, Plus forts dans

l'u - ni - té, chaqu' jour à la tâ - che, Pour la

pos - té - ri - té, cons - trui - sez sans re - lâ - che.

2. *Quand partout souffle un vent de colère et de haine,*
   Béninois, sois fier, et d'une âme sereine,
   Confiant dans l'avenir, regarde ton drapeau!
   Dans le vert tu liras l'espoir du renouveau,
   De tes aïeux le rouge évoque le courage;
   Des plus riches trésors le jaune est le présage.

   CHORUS

72

3. *Tes monts ensoleillés, tes palmiers, ta verdure,*
   Cher Bénin, partout font ta vive parure.
   Ton sol offre à chacun la richesse des fruits.
   Bénin, désormais que tes fils tous unis
   D'un fraternel élan partagent l'espérance
   De te voir à jamais heureux dans l'abondance.

CHORUS

Translation by Elizabeth P. Coleman

1. Formerly, at her call, our ancestors
   Knew how to engage in mighty battles
   With strength, courage, ardour, and full of joy, but at the price of blood.
   Builders of the present, you too, join forces
   Each day for the task stronger in unity.
   Build without ceasing for posterity.

   CHORUS
   Children of Bénin, arise!
   The resounding cry of freedom
   Is heard at the first light of dawn;
   Children of Bénin, arise!

2. When all around there blows a wind of anger and hate:
   Citizen of Bénin, be proud, and in a calm spirit
   Trusting in the future, behold your flag!
   In the green you read hope of spring;
   The red signifies the courage of your ancestors;
   The yellow foretells the richest treasures.

   CHORUS

3. Beloved Bénin, your sunny mountains, palm trees, and green pastures
   Show everywhere your brightness;
   Your soil offers everyone the richest fruits.
   Bénin, from henceforth your sons are united
   With one brotherly spirit sharing the hope of seeing you
   Enjoy abundance and happiness for ever.

   CHORUS

BHUTAN

Words by
GYALDUN DASHO THINLEY DORJI (1914 - 1966)

Music by
DASHO AKU TONGMI (*b*. 1913)

Adopted in 1953.

Translation

Druk Tsen-dhen Koe-pai Gyal-khab-na.
Pal Lug-nyi Ten-sid Kyong-wai Goen.
Druk Gyalpo Nga-dhag Rinpoche.
Ku Gyur-med Ten-ching Chhab-sid Phel.
Chhoe Sangye Ten-pa Dhar-zhing gye.
Bang Dhe-kid Nyi-ma Shar-war Sho.

In the thunder dragon Kingdom, adorned with sandal woods,
The protector who guards the teachings of the dual system,
He, the precious and glorious ruler, causes dominion to spread,
While his unchanging person abides in constancy,
As the doctrine of the Lord Buddha flourishes,
May the sun of peace and happiness shine on the people.

BOLIVIA
Canción Patriotica
(Patriotic Song)

Words by
JOSÉ IGNACIO DE SANJINÉS (1786 - 1864)

Music by
LEOPOLDO BENEDETTO VINCENTI (1815 - 1914)

1. Bo - li - via - nos: el ha - do pro -
pi - cio Co - ro - nó — nues - tros vo - tos y an - he - lo; Es ya

Played for the first time in 1842 and adopted the same year.

li - bre ya li - bre es - te sue — lo, Ya — ce - só su - ser - vil — con - di -

ción.   Al es - truen - do mar - cial que a - yer fue — ra Y al cla -

mor — de la gue - rra ho - rro - ro - so, Si - guen hoy — en con - tras - te ar - mo -

nio - so Dul - ces him - nos de paz — y — de u - nion.   Si - guen

hoy— en con-tras-te_ar-mo-nio — so Dul-ces him-nos de paz— y—de u-

nion. De la Pa-tria, el al-to nom — bre En glo-

rio-so_es-plen-dor— con-ser-ve — mos, Y_en sus a — ras de nue-vo ju-

re - mos, ¡Mo - rir an - tes que_es - cla - vos vi - vir! ¡Mo - rir

marcato

an - tes que_es - cla - vos vi - vir! ¡Mo - rir an - tes que_es - cla - vos vi -

vir!

sf

2. *Aqui alzó la justicia su trono,*
   Que la vil opresión desconoca.
   Y este timbre glorioso legóse.
   Libertad! Libertad! Libertad!
   Que los hijos del grande Bolívar
   Han ya mil y mil veces jurado,
   Morir antes que ver humillado
   De la Patria el augusto pendón.

   CHORUS

3. *Loor eterno a los bravos guerreros*
   Cuyo heroico valor y firmeza
   Conquistaron las glorias que empieza.
   Hoy Bolivia feliz a gozar.
   Que sus nombres el mármol y el bronce
   A remotas edades trasmitan
   Y en sonoros cantares repitan
   Nuestros hijos y nietos a par.

   CHORUS

Translation by T. M. Cartledge

1. Bolivians, a favourable destiny
   Has crowned our vows and longings;
   This land is free,
   Your servile state has ended.
   The martial turmoil of yesterday
   And the horrible clamour of war
   Are followed today, in harmonious contrast, } (twice)
   By sweet hymns of peace and unity.

   CHORUS

   We have kept the lofty name of our country
   In glorious splendour,
   And on its altars we once more swear
   To die, rather than live as slaves.   } (three times)

2. This innocent and beautiful land,
   Which owes its name to Bol var,
   Is the happy homeland where men
   Enjoy the benefits of good fortune and peace.
   For the sons of the great Bol var
   Have sworn, thousands upon thousands of times,
   To die rather than see the country's } (twice)
   Majestic flag humiliated.

   CHORUS

3. Eternal praise to the brave warriors
   Whose heroic valour and firmness
   Conquered the glories that now
   A happy Bolivia begins to enjoy!
   Let their names, in marble and in bronze,
   Transmit to remote ages
   And in resounding song repeat the call: } (twice)
   Freedom! Freedom! Freedom!

   CHORUS

BOSNIA AND HERZEGOVINA
Intermeco
(Intermezzo)

No words

Music by
DUŠAN ŠESTIC (b. 1946)
Arr. by MARTIN WEHN

Adopted in 1998.

BOTSWANA

Words and music by
KGALEMANG TUMEDISCO MOTSETE (1900 - 1974)
Arr. by W. L. REED

Officially adopted on 30 September, 1966.

mang - ba - sa - di, e - mang, tlha - ga - fa - lang! Re ko -
wo - men close be - side them stand, To -

pa - ne - leng go di - re - la Le - fat - she la ro - na.
ge - ther we'll work and serve This land, this hap - py land!

2. *Ina lentle la tumo*
   La chaba ya Botswana,
   Ka kutlwano le kagisano,
   E bopagantswe mmogo.

CHORUS

Translation

2. Word of beauty and of fame,
   The name Botswana to us came.
   Through our unity and harmony,
   We'll remain at peace as one.

CHORUS

BRAZIL

Words by
JOAQUIM OSÓRIO DUQUE ESTRADA (1870 - 1927)

Music by
FRANCISCO MANOEL DA SILVA (1795 - 1865)

The music was written in 1831 on the accession of Emperor Dom Pedro II.
In 1922 a new text was officially adopted and the same tune retained.

1. Ou - vi - ram do I - pi - ran - ga às mar - gens plá - ci - das De um po - vo he - rói - co o bra - do re - tum - ban - te, E o Sol da li - ber - da - de em ra - ios fúl - gi - dos, Bri - lhou no céu da Pá - tria nes - se in-

stan - te, Se o pe - nhor_____ des - sa i - gual - da - de Con - se -
gui - mos con - quis - tar com bra - ço for - te, Em teu
sei - o, ó, Li - ber - da - de, De - sa -
fi - a o nos - so pei - to a pró - pria mor - te! Ó Pá - tria a -

ma - gem do Cru - zei - ro res - plan - de - ce. Gi -

gan - te pe - la pró - pria na - tu - re - za, És

be - lo, és for - te, im - pá - vi - do co - los - so. E o

teu fu - tu - ro es - pe - lha es - sa gran - de - za! Ter - ra a - do -

ra - da, En - tre ou - tras mil, És tu, Bra - sil, Ó Pá - tria a -

ma - da! Dos fi - lhos des - te so - lo és mãe gen -

til, Pá - tria a - ma - da, Bra - sil!

sil!

2. *Deitado eternamente em berço esplêndido,*
   Ao som do mar e à luz do céu profundo,
   Fulguras, ó Brasil, florão da América,
   Iluminado ao sol do novo mundo!
   Do que a terra mais garrida
   Teus risonhos, lindos campos têm mais flores;
   "Nossos bosques têm mais vida,"
   "Nossa vida" no teu seio "mais amores."

   Ó Pátria amada, Idolatrada, Salve! Salve!

   Brasil, de amor eterno seja o símbolo
   O lábaro que ostentas estrelado,
   E diga o verde-louro dessa flâmula:
   "Paz no futuro e glória no passado."
   Mas, se ergues da justiça a clava forte,
   Verás que um filho teu não foge à luta
   Nem teme, quem te adora, a própria morte.

   CHORUS
   Terra adorada, Entre outras mil, Es tu, Brasil,
   Ó Pátria amada! Dos filhos deste solo és mãe gentil,
   Pátria amada, Brasil!

1. There was heard, from Ypiranga's placid banks,
   The resounding cry of a heroic people,
   And the sun of freedom, in bright rays,
   Shone at this moment in the homeland's skies.
   As the promise of this equality
   Was secured by our strong arms,
   In your bosom, O Freedom,
   We are ready to die.

   O beloved, idolized homeland, hail, hail!
   Brazil, a vivid dream, a lively ray
   Of love and hope settles on the earth,
   As in your beautiful sky, smiling and limpid,
   The image of the Southern Cross shines resplendent.
   A giant by nature, you are beautiful,
   Strong, an intrepid colossus,
   And your future mirrors this grandeur.

   CHORUS
   O land we adore, among a thousand others
   You are the beloved one.
   You are the gentle mother of the sons of this land,
   Beloved homeland, Brazil!

2. Eternally laid in a splendid cradle,
   To the sound of the sea and the light from the depths of the sky,
   Brazil, you gleam, fleuron of the Americas,
   Illuminated by the sun of the New World.
   Your smiling, lovely fields have more flowers
   Than the most attractive land elsewhere,
   Our forests have more life,
   Our life in your bosom more love.

   O beloved, idolized homeland, hail, hail!
   Brazil, may you have as eternal symbol
   The starry banner you display,
   And may the green laurel of this pennant speak
   Of peace in the future and glory in the past.
   But if you raise a strong cudgel in the name of justice,
   You will see that a son of yours does not run from a fight,
   Nor does one who adores you fear death.

   CHORUS

BRUNEI DARUSSALAM

Words by
PENGIRAN HAJI MOHAMED YUSUF BIN
ABDUL RAHIM (*b*. 1923)

Music by
AWANG HAJI BESAR BIN SAGAP (1914 - 1988)

Composed in 1947 through the initiative of a group of youths who decided that their country should have a National Anthem, and chose two of their number to write and compose it. It was officially adopted in 1951. The country became independent on 1 January, 1984.

94

Hi - dup sen - to - sa Ne - ga - ra dan Sul - tan, I - la - hi se - la-

mat - kan Bru - nei Da - rus - sa - lam.

Translation

Oh God, Long live our Majesty the Sultan;
Justice and Sovereignty in sheltering
Our country and leading our people;
Prosperity to our Nation and Sultan.
God save Brunei Darussalam.

BULGARIA
Mila Rodino
(Dear Homeland)

Words and music by
TSVETAN TSVETKOV RADOSLAVOV (1863 - 1931)

Original words and music were composed by Radoslavov while still a student in 1885, and on his way to fight in the Serbo-Bulgarian War. It quickly became popular. It was arranged as the National Anthem, replacing the previous Communist Anthem in 1964.

There is a longer version, but the above is the one that is usually sung.

Translation by Katya Boyadjieva

Proudly rise the Balkan peaks,
At their feet Blue Danube flows;
Over Thrace the sun is shining,
Pirin looms in purple glow.

CHORUS
Oh, dear native land,
Earthly paradise!
For your loveliness, your beauty
E'er will charm our eyes.
} (twice)

BURKINA FASO
Une Seule Nuit
(One Single Night)

Words by
THOMAS SANKARA (1949 - 1987)

Composer unknown
Arr. by W. L. REED

Adopted on 2 August, 1984. The change of name from Upper Volta to Burkina Faso took place in August, 1984.

1. *Contre la férule humiliante il y a déjà mille ans,*
   La rapacité venue de loin les asservir il y a cent ans.
   Contre la cynique malice métamorphosée
   En néocolonialisme et ses petits servants locaux
   Beaucoup flanchèrent et certains résistèrent.
   Mais les échecs, les succès, la sueur, le sang
   Ont fortifié notre peuple courageux et fertilisé sa lutte héroïque.

   CHORUS
   Et une seule nuit a rassemblé en elle
   L'histoire de tout un peuple.
   Et une seule nuit a déclenché sa marche triomphale
   Vers l'horizon du bonheur.
   Une seule nuit a réconcilié notre peuple
   Avec tous les peuples du monde,
   A la conquête de la liberté et du progrès
   La Patrie ou la mort, nous vaincrons.

2. *Nourris à la source vive de la Révolution,*
   Les engagés volontaires de la liberté et de la paix
   Dans l'energie nocturne et salutaire du 4 août
   N'avaient pas que les armes à la main, mais aussi et surtout
   La flamme au cœur pour legitimement libérer
   Le Faso à jamais des fers de tous ceux qui
   Çà et là en poluaient l'âme sacrée de l'indépendance, de la souveraineté.

   CHORUS

3. *Et séant désormais en sa dignité recouvrée*
   L'amour et l'honneur en partage avec l'humanité,
   Le peuple du Burkina chante un hymne à la victoire,
   A la gloire du travail libérateur, émancipateur.
   A bas l'exploitation de l'homme par l'homme!
   Hé en avant pour le bonheur de tout homme,
   Par tous les hommes aujourd'hui et demain, par tous les hommes ici et pour toujours!

   CHORUS

4. *Révolution populaire notre sève nourricière.*
   Maternité immortelle du progrès à visage d'homme.
   Foyer éternel de démocratie consensuelle,
   Où enfin l'identité nationale a droit de cité,
   Où pour toujours l'injustice perd ses quartiers,
   Et où, des mains des bâtisseurs d'un monde radieux
   Mûrissent partout les moissons de vœux patriotiques, brillent les soleils infinis de joie.

   CHORUS

Translation by K. Jonathan Fryer

1. Against the humiliating bondage of a thousand years
    Rapacity came from afar to subjugate them for a hundred years.
    Against the cynical malice in the shape
    Of neo-colonialism and its petty local servants,
    Many gave in and certain others resisted.
    But the frustrations, the successes, the sweat, the blood
    Have fortified our courageous people and fertilised its heroic struggle.

    CHORUS
    And one single night has drawn together
    The history of an entire people,
    And one single night has launched its triumphal march
    Towards the horizon of good fortune.
    One single night has brought together our people
    With all the peoples of the World,
    In the acquisition of liberty and progress.
    Motherland or death, we shall conquer.

2. Nourished in the lively source of the Revolution,
    The volunteers for liberty and peace
    With their nocturnal and beneficial energies of the 4th of August
    Had not only hand arms, but also and above all
    The flame in their hearts lawfully to free
    Faso forever from the fetters of all those who
    Here and there were polluting the sacred soul of independence and sovereignty.

    CHORUS

3. And seated henceforth in rediscovered dignity,
    Love and honour partnered with humanity,
    The people of Burkina sing a victory hymn
    To the glory of the work of liberation and emancipation.
    Down with exploitation of man by man!
    Forward for the good of every man
    By all men of today and tomorrow, by every man here and always!

    CHORUS

4. Popular revolution our nourishing sap,
    Undying motherhood of progress in the face of man.
    Eternal hearth of agreed democracy,
    Where at last national identity has the right to freedom,
    Where injustice has lost its place forever,
    And where from the hands of builders of a glorious world
    Everywhere harvests of patriotic vows ripen and suns of boundless joy shine.

    CHORUS

BURUNDI

Words by
JEAN-BAPTISTE NTAHOKAJA (*b.* 1920)

Music prepared by
MARC BARENGAYABO (*b.* 1934)
Arr. by W. L. REED

Bu - rŭ - ndi bwâ - cu, Bu - rŭ - ndi bu - hĭ - re,

Shī - ngai - cú - mu mu ma - shī - nga, Ga - bai - ntă - he y'ú - bu - ga - bo

ku bu - gī - ngo. Wa - rá - pfu - nywe ntí - wa - pfû - ye,

Adopted in June 1962.

102

twē - se, Tu - gu - tū - ye a - ma - bó - ko, u - mí - ti - ma

n'ú - bu - zi - ma, I - mâ - na ya - kú - du - hā - ye i - ku - dú -

tū - ngi - re. Ho - ra - na um - wă - mi n'á - ba - ga - bo n'í - tĕ - kā - ne.

Sā - gwa n'ú - rwĕ - ze, sā - gwa n'á - ma - hó - ro mē - zá.

Cher Burundi, ô doux pays,
Prends place dans le concert des nations.
En tout bien, tout honneur, accédé à l'indépendance,
Mutilé et meutri, tu es demeuré maître de toi-même.

L'heure venue, tu t'es levé
Et fièrement tu t'es hissé au rang des peuples libres.
Reçois donc le compliment des nations,
Agrée l'hommage de tes enfants.
Qu'à travers l'univers retentisse ton nom.

Cher Burundi, héritage sacré de nos aïeux,
Reconnu digne de te gouverner,
Au courage tu allies le sentiment de l'honneur.
Chante la gloire de ta liberté reconquise.

Cher Burundi, digne objet de notre plus tendre amour,
A ton noble service nous vouons nos bras, nos cœurs et nos vies.
Veuille Dieu, qui nous a fait don de toi, te conserver à notre vénération,
Sous l'égide de l'Unité,
Dans la paix, la joie et la prospérité.

Translation (of French Version) by T. M. Cartledge

Beloved Burundi, gentle country,
Take your place in the concert of nations,
Acceding to independence with honourable intentions.
Wounded and bruised, you have remained master of yourself.

When the hour came, you arose,
Lifting yourself proudly into the ranks of free peoples.
Receive, then, the congratulations of the nations
And the homage of your sons.
May your name ring out through the universe.

Beloved Burundi, sacred heritage from our forefathers,
Recognised as worthy of self-government,
With your courage you also have a sense of honour.
Sing the glory of liberty conquered again.

Beloved Burundi, worthy of our tenderest love,
We vow to your noble service our hands and hearts and lives.
May God, who gave you to us, keep you for us to venerate,
Under the shield of unity,
In peace, joy and prosperity.

CAMBODIA
Nokoreach

Words by
CHUON NAT (1883 - 1969)

Composer unknown*
Arr. by W. L. REED

1. Som pouk tep - da rak sa moha khsath yeung⸺ oy ben roung roeung doy chey mon - kol⸺ srey sour - sdey Yeung Khnom preah ang som chrok Krom moloup preah Ba - ro -

Originally adopted in 1941, reaffirmed in 1947, replaced in 1976 and restored on 21 September, 1993.

* Adapted from a Cambodian folk song.

2. *Prasath séla kombang kan dal prey*
   Kuor oy srâmay noeuk dâl yuos sak Moha Nokor
   Cheat Khmer dauch Thmar kong vong nây lâar rung peung chom hor.
   Yeung sang Khim por pheap preng samnang robuos Kampuchea.
   Moha râth koeut mień you ang veanh hey.

3. *Kroup vath aram lû tè so sap thoeur*
   Sot doy am nô rom lik koun poth sasna
   Chol yeung chea neak thioeur thiak smos smak tam bêp donnta
   Kong tè thévoda nùng chuoy chrom chrèng phkôt phkang pra yoch oy
   Dol prateah Khmer chea Moha Nokor.

French Translation

1. *Que le ciel protège notre Roi*
   Et lui dispense le bonheur et la gloire.
   Qu'il règne sur nos cœurs et sur nos destinées,
   Celui qui, héritier des Souverains bâtisseurs,
   Gouverne le fier et vieux Royaume.

2. *Les temples dorment dans la forêt,*
   Rappelant la grandeur du Moha Nokor.
   Comme le roc, la race khmère est éternelle,
   Ayons confiance dans le sort du Campuchéa,
   L'Empire qui défie les années.

3. *Les chants montent dans le pagodes*
   A la gloire de la Sainte foi Bouddhique.
   Soyons fidèles aux croyances de nos pères.
   Ainsi le ciel prodiguera-t-il tous ses bienfaits
   Au vieux pays khmer, le Moha Nokor.

English Translation

1. Heaven protects our King
   And gives him happiness and glory
   To reign over our souls and our destinies,
   The one being, heir of the Sovereign builders,
   Guiding the proud old Kingdom.

2. Temples are asleep in the forest,
   Remembering the splendour of Moha Nokor.
   Like a rock the Khmer race is eternal.
   Let us trust in the fate of Campuchea,
   The empire which challenges the ages.

3. Songs rise up from the pagodas
   To the glory of holy buddhistic faith.
   Let us be faithful to our ancestors' belief.
   Thus heaven will lavish its bounty
   Towards the ancient Khmer country, the Moha Nokor.

CAMEROON
Chant de Ralliement
(Song of Reunification)

Words by
RENÉ DJAM AFAME (1910 - 1981)
English versification by
T. M. CARTLEDGE

Music by
RENÉ DJAM AFAME (1910 - 1981)
SAMUEL MINKIO BAMBA (*b.* 1911)
and MOÏSE NYATTE NKO'O (1910 - 1978)
Arr. by HENRY COLEMAN

Tempo di marcia

1. O Ca - me - roun, ber - ceau de nos an - cê - tres, Va, de - bout, et ja - loux de ta li - ber - té. Comme un so - leil, ton dra - peau fier doit ê - tre Un sym -

1. O Ca - me - roon, thou cra - dle of our fa - thers, Proud - ly ral - ly to de - fend your lib - er - ty. And like the sun, your flag will be re - splend - ent, As a

Adopted as the unofficial National Anthem in 1948, it became the official National Anthem on 10 May, 1957. The words were substantially changed in 1978.

bole ar - dent de foi et d'u - ni - té._____ Que_____
sym - bol of your faith and u - ni - ty._____ May_____

tous tes en - fants du___ Nord au Sud, De_____
all your chil - dren fol - low the com - mand, From_____

l'Est à l'Ou - est soient tout a - mour!_____ Te ser - vir
East and___ West to give their heart,_____ Their on - ly

que ce soit___ leur___ seul___ but Pour___
wish___ to___ serve___ their___ land And___ with

CHORUS

rem - plir leur de - voir tou - jours.
con - stan - cy play their part.

Chère Pa - tri - e, terre ché - ri - e, Tu
This our land that we all love so, On

es no - tre seul et vrai bon - heur.
you our whole hap - pi - ness is stayed.

No - tre
You're our

joie et no - tre vi - e, A toi l'a -
joy and you're our life too; To you be

mour et le grand hon - neur.
hon - our and love dis - played.

25

2. *Tu es la tombe où dorment nos pères,*
 Le jardin que nos aïeux ont cultivé.
 Nous travaillons pour te rendre prospère,
 Un beau jour enfin nous serons arrivés.
 De l'Afrique sois fidèle enfant
 Et progresse toujours en paix,
 Espérant que tes jeunes enfants
 T'aimeront sans bornes à jamais.

 CHORUS

2. You are the tomb where our fathers are resting,
 You're the garden they prepared and they conceived,
 We work that you may become fair and prosp'rous,
 And one day at last we'll see it all achieved.
 May you be a faithful child of Africa,
 Advancing steadily in peace,
 In hope that ev'ry young child of yours
 Will love you until time shall cease.

 CHORUS

CANADA

French words by
SIR ADOLPHE BASILE ROUTHIER (1839 - 1920)
English words by
ROBERT STANLEY WEIR (1856 - 1926)

Music by
CALIXA LAVALLÉE (1842 - 1891)
Arr. by W. L. REED

Maestoso
VERSE

mf
1. O Ca - na - da! Ter - re de nos aï - eux,
1. O Ca - na - da! Our home and na - tive land!

Ton front est ceint de fleur - ons glo - ri - eux! Car ton
True pa - triot love in all thy sons com - mand. With—

bras sait por - ter l'é - pé - e, Il— sait por - ter la
glow - ing hearts we— see thee rise, The— True North strong and

Officially adopted on 1 July, 1980.

2. Sous l'œil de Dieu, près du fleuve géant,
   Le Canadien grandit en espérant.
   Il est né d'une race fière,
   Béni fut son berceau,
   Le ciel a marqué sa carriére,
   Dans ce monde nouveau.

CHORUS

2. O Canada! Where pines and maples grow,
   Great prairies spread and lordly rivers flow,
   How dear to us thy broad domain,
   From East to Western sea!
   Thou land of hope for all who toil!
   Thou True North strong and free!

CHORUS

CAPE VERDE

Cântico da Liberdade
(Song of Freedom)

Words by
AMILCAR SPENCER LOPES (*b.* 1948)

Music by
ADALBERTO HIGINO TAVARES SILVA (*b.* 1961)
Arr. by GILBERT de GREEVE

Adopted on 5 July, 1996.

pó da il - ha nu — a. No des - pe - nha - dei - ro da vi - da A es -

pe — ran - ça é do ta - ma — nho do mar que nos a -

bra - ça—— Sen - ti - ne - la de ma - res e ven - tos per - se - ve -

hi - no e͜o Ho - mem a cer - te - za!

Translation by Terry Roberts

Sing, brother
Sing, my brother
That Liberty is an anthem
And that Man the certainty.

With dignity, plant the seed
In the dust of the bare island:
In the precipice of life
Hope is the size of the sea
That embraces us.
Guardian of the seas and winds
Persevering
Between stars and the Atlantic
She sings the hymn of Liberty.

Sing, brother
Sing, my brother
That Liberty is an anthem
And that Man the certainty.

CENTRAL AFRICAN REPUBLIC
La Renaissance
(The Rebirth)

Words by
BARTHÉLÉMY BOGANDA (1910 - 1959)

Music by
HERBERT PEPPER (1912 - 2001) *

O Cen - tra - fri - que, ô ber - ceau des Ban - tous! Re - prends ton droit au res - pect, à la vie! Long - temps sou - mis, long - temps bri - mé par tous, Mais de ce jour bri -

Adopted on 25 May, 1960.
* Herbert Pepper also wrote the music of the National Anthem of Sénégal.

sant la ty - ran - nie. Dans le tra-vail, l'ordre et la di - gni - té,

Tu re - con - quiers ton droit, ton u - ni - té, Et pour fran - chir cette

é - ta - pe nou - vel - le, De nos an - cê - tres la voix— nous ap - pel - le.

CHORUS

f

Au tra - vail dans l'ordre et la di - gni - té, Dans le res - pect du

f

droit dans l'u - ni - té, Bri - sant la mi - sè - re et la ty - ran - nie,

Bran - diss - ant l'é - ten - dard_____ de la Pa - trie._____

Translation by T. M. Cartledge

Oh! Central Africa, cradle of the Bantu!
Take up again your right to respect, to life!
Long subjugated, long scorned by all,
But, from today, breaking tyranny's hold.
Through work, order and dignity
You reconquer your rights, your unity,
And to take this new step
The voice of our ancestors calls us.

CHORUS
To work! In order and dignity,
In the respect for rights and in unity,
Breaking poverty and tyranny,
Holding high the flag of the Fatherland.

CHAD
La Tchadienne
(The Song of Chad)

Words by
LOUIS GIDROL (*b.* 1922) *
and students of St. Paul's School

Music by
PAUL VILLARD (1899 - 1986)
Arr. by Col. P. DUPONT

Peu - ple Tcha - dien, de - bout et à l'ou - vra - ge! Tu as con-
quis ta terre et ton droit; Ta li - ber - té naî-

Composed for the proclamation of independence in January, 1960.
* Year of death unknown.

yeux, pa - ci - fique, a - vance en chan - tant, Fi - dèle à tes an -

ciens qui te re - gar - dent.

D. %al Fine

Translation by T. M. Cartledge

CHORUS
People of Chad, arise and take up the task!
You have conquered the soil and won your rights;
Your freedom will be born of your courage.
Lift up your eyes, the future is yours.

VERSE
Oh, my Country, may God protect you,
May your neighbours admire your children.
Joyful, peaceful, advance as you sing,
Faithful to your fathers who are watching you.

CHORUS

CHILE

Words by
EUSEBIO LILLO ROBLES (1826 - 1910)
and BERNARDO DE VERA Y PINTADO (1789 - 1826)

Music by
RAMÓN CARNICER Y BATTLE (1780 - 1855)

The music was adopted on 17 September, 1847, the words on 12 August, 1909 and it was recognised officially on 27 June, 1941. There are six verses.

co - pia fe - liz_____ del E - dén. Ma - jes -

tuo - sa es la blan - ca mon - ta - ña Que te

dió por ba - luar - te el Se - ñor, Que te

dió por ba - luar - te el Se - ñor, Y e - se

mar _____ que tran - qui - lo te ba - ña Te pro -

me - te fu - tu - ro es - plen - dor, _____ Y _____ e - se

mar _____ que tran - qui - lo _____ te ba - ña Te _____ pro -

me - te _____ fu - tu - ro es - plen - dor.

cresc.

tum - ba se - rás de los li - bres O el a -

si - lo con - tra la o - pre - sión, Que o la

tum - ba se - rás de los li - bres O el a -

si - lo con - tra la o - pre - sión, Que o la tum - ba se - rás de los

li - bres   O͜ el   a - si - lo   con - tra   la o͜ - pre -

sión,   O͜ el   a - si - lo con - tra   la o͜ - pre -

sión,   O͜ el   a - si - lo con - tra   la o͜ - pre -

sión.

ff

2. *Vuestros nombres, valientes soldados*
   Que habéis sido de Chile el sostén,
   Nuestros pechos los llevan grabados;
   Lo sabrán nuestros hijos también.
   Sean ellos el grito de muerte
   Que lancemos marchando a lidiar,   } (twice)
   Y, sonando en la boca del fuerte,
   Hagan siempre al tirano temblar.   } (twice)

   CHORUS

Translation by T. M. Cartledge

1. Chile, your sky is a pure blue,
   Pure breezes blow across you,
   And your field, embroidered with flowers,
   Is a happy copy of Eden.
   Majestic is the snow-covered mountain
   That was given to you by the Lord as a bastion, } (twice)
   And the sea that tranquilly washes your shore
   Promises future splendour for you.   } (twice)

   CHORUS
   Gentle homeland, accept the vows
   Given, Chile, on your altars,
   That you be either the tomb of the free   } (three times)
   Or a refuge from oppression.   } (twice)

2. Your names, gallant soldiers
   Who have been Chile's support,
   Will be carried engraved on our hearts;
   Our sons shall know this too.
   May they be the battle cry
   Uttered as we march into combat,   } (twice)
   And, resounding in the mouth of the strong,
   May they ever make the tyrant tremble.   } (twice)

   CHORUS

CHINA
March of the Volunteers

Words by
TIAN HAN (1898 - 1968)

Music by
NIE ER (1912 - 1935)

This song was written in 1935. On 27 September, 1949 it was officially approved as the National Anthem. New words were adopted on 5 March, 1978, but in 1982 the original words were restored.

pao   hŭo.   Qian   jin!   Qian   jin!   Qian   jin!   Jin!

33

Translation

Arise, ye who refuse to be slaves!
With our flesh and blood, let us build our new Great Wall!
The Chinese nation faces its greatest danger.
From each one the urgent call for action comes forth.
Arise! Arise! Arise!
Millions with but one heart,
Braving the enemy's fire.
March on!
Braving the enemy's fire.
March on ! March on! March on! On!

COLOMBIA

Words by
RAFAEL NÚÑEZ (1825 - 1894)

Music by
ORESTE SINDICI (1837 - 1904)

¡Oh gloria in - mar - ce - si - ble! ¡Oh júbilo in - mor - tal! En

Officially adopted on 4 July, 1946. First sung on 11 November, 1887 in Bogotá. There are eleven verses.

VERSE (Solo)

1. Ce - só la ho-rri - ble___ no - che, La li - ber - tad___ su -
bli - me De - rra - ma las___ au - ro - ras
De su in - ven - ci - ble luz. La hu - ma - ni - dad en -
te - ra, Que en - tre ca - de - nas gi - me, Com -

pren - de las pa - la - bras Del que mu - rió en la Cruz.

39

2. 'Independencia' grita
   El mundo americano;
   Se bãna en sangre de héroes
   La tierra de Colón.
   Pero este gran principio:
   'El Rey no es soberano',
   Resuena, y los que sufren
   Bendicen su pasión.

   CHORUS

Translation

CHORUS
Oh unfading glory!
Oh immortal joy!
In furrows of pain   } (twice)
Good is already germinating.

1. The fearful night came to an end,
   Liberty sublime
   Is spreading the dawns
   Of its invincible light.
   The whole of humanity,
   Which is groaning under chains,
   Understands the words
   Of the One who died on the Cross.

   CHORUS

2. 'Independence' cries
   The American world;
   In heroes' blood is bathing
   The Land of Columbus.
   But this great principle:
   'The King is not sovereign',
   Resounds, and those who suffer
   Praise the passion in it.

   CHORUS

THE COMOROS
Udzima wa ya Masiwa
(The Union of the Great Islands)

Words by
SAID HACHIM SIDI ABDEREMANE (*b.* 1942)

Music by
KAMILDINE ABDALLAH (1943 - 1982) and
SAID HACHIM SIDI ABDEREMANE (*b.* 1942)
Arr. by W. L. REED

Con spirito

I béra - mu i - si pé - pé - za i na - di ukom - bo-zi pi-
mu i - si pé - pé - za ra - ngu mwési si - ta wa Zui-

ya i dau - la i - vé - nu - ha ta-
ye i dau - la i - vé - nu - ha zi

si - ba bu ya i di - ni vo - ya tra - nga -
si - wa za - tru zi pa - ngwi ha Ma - o - ré na Nzu - a -

Adopted in 1978.

ya   hu - nu Ko - mo - ri - ya———   Na - ri - ké - ni———————   na ma - ha-
ni,   Mwa - li - na Nga - zi - ya———   Na - ri - ké - ni———————   na ma - ha-

1.
ba   ya   hu - vein - dza ya ma - si - wa———   ya - tru

ff
wa - si - wa Ko - mo - ro   da - mu   ndzi - ma

ff

wa - si - wa Ko - mo - ro   di - ni ndzi - ma   Ya ma - si - wa ra - dza - li wa

ya ma-si-wa ya-ri-le-ya Mo-la né a-ri sa-yi-di-ya

Na-ri-ké-ni ha ni-ya ri-vein-dzé uwa-ta-ni-ya

Ma-ha-ba ya di-ne na du-ni-ya. I béra-

ba___ ya hu-vein-dzar ya ma-si-wa.

Au faîte le Drapeau flotte
Appelle à la Liberté totale.
La nation apparaît,
Force d'une même religion au sein des Comores.
Vivons dans l'amour réciproque dans nos îles.

Les Comoriens issue de même sang,
Nous embrassons la même idéologie réligieuse.
Les îles où nous sommes nés.
Les îles qui nous ont prodigués la bonne éducation.
Dieu y a apporté son aide.
Conservons notre unité pour l'amour de la patrie,
Amour pour la réligion
Et pour l'évolution.

Au faîte le Drapeau flotte
Depuis le 6 du mois de Juillet
La nation apparaît,
Les îles devenues souveraines;
Maore—N'Dzouani—Mouwali—et N'Gazidja.
Gardons notre amour pour les îles.

English Translation by Jan Knappert

The flag is flying,
Announcing complete independence;
The nation rises up
Because of the faith we have
In this our Comoria.

Let us always have devotion
To love our Great Islands.
We Comorians are of one blood,
We Comorians are of one faith.

On these Islands we were born,
These Islands brought us up.
May God always help us;
Let us always have the firm resolve
To love our fatherland,
Love our religion and the world.

The flag is flying.
From the Sixth of July
The Nation rises up;
Our Islands are lined up.
Maori and Anzuan, Moheli and Comore,
Let us always have devotion
To love our Great Islands.

CONGO (DEMOCRATIC REPUBLIC)
Debout Kongolaise
(Arise Congolese)

Words and music by
SIMON-PIERRE BOKA (*b.* 1929)

Replaced on 17 May, 1997, when the county's former name, Zaïre, was changed.

Don bé - ni, Con - go, des a - ïux, Con - go, O pa -

ys, Con - go, bien ai - mé, Con - go, Nous peu - ple - rons ton sol Et nous as - su - re -

rons ta gran - deur. Tren - te juin, ô doux so - leil, Tren - te juin du tren - te juin, jour sa -

cré, Sois le té - moin, jour sa - cré, de l'im - mor - tel ser - ment de li - ber - té

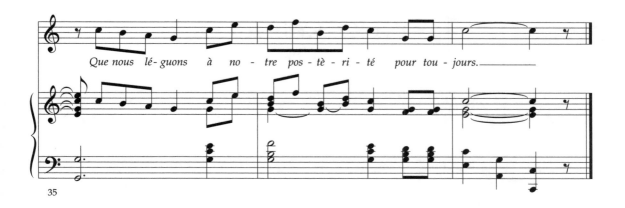

Que nous lé- guons   à   no - tre pos - tè - ri - té   pour tou - jours.

35

Translation by W. L. Reed

Rise up Congolese, united in destiny,
United in the fight for independence.
Raise your heads, which were bent low for so long
And leap into a great future.
In peace, ardent people,
Through your efforts, we shall build
A more beautiful country than before, in peace.

Citizens, strike up the sacred hymn of your solidarity.
Proudly salute the golden emblem of your sovereignty – Congo!

CHORUS
Congo, blessed gift of your forefathers, Congo!
Congo, our much loved country,
We shall populate your land
And we shall secure your greatness.
June the Thirtieth, sweet sun,
Great June the Thirtieth, sacred day!
Be the witness, sacred day, of everlasting declaration of Liberty,
Which we shall bequeath to posterity for ever.

CONGO (REPUBLIC)

La Congolaise
(The Song of Congo)

Words by
LEVENT KIMBANGUI *

Music by
FRANÇAIS JACQUES TONDRA *
Arr. by HENRY COLEMAN

1. En ce jour le so-leil se lè - ve Et no-tre Con-go res-plen-dit. U-ne lon-gue nuit s'a-chè - ve, Un grand bon-heur a sur - gi. Chan - tons

Officially adopted in 1962, replaced in 1969 and restored on 10 June, 1991.
* Dates not yet available.

tous a - vec i - vres - se le chant de la li - ber -

CHORUS

té. Con - go - lais, de - bout fiè - re -

ment par - tout, Pro - cla - mons l'u - nion de no - tre na - tion, Ou - bli -

ons ce qui nous di - vi - se, so - yons plus u - nis que ja -

2. Des forêts jusqu'à la savanne,
   Des savannes jusqu'à la mer,
   Un seul peuple, une seule âme,
   Un seul cœur, ardent et fier,
   Luttons tous, tant que nous sommes,
   Pour notre vieux pays noir.

   CHORUS

3. Et s'il nous faut mourir, en somme
   Qu'importe puisque nos enfants,
   Partout, pourront dire comme
   On triomphe en combattant,
   Et dans le moindre village
   Chantent sous nos trois couleurs.

   CHORUS

1. On this day the sun rises
   And our Congo stands resplendent.
   A long night is ended,
   A great happiness has come.
   Let us all, with wild joyfulness, sing
   The song of freedom.

   CHORUS
   Arise, Congolese, proud every man,
   Proclaim the unity of our nation.
   Let us forget what divides us
   And become more united than ever.
   Let us live our motto:
   Unity, work, progress.
   Let us live our motto:
   Unity, work, progress.

2. From the forest to the bush,
   From the bush to the ocean,
   One people, one soul,
   One heart, ardent and proud.
   Let us all fight, every one of us,
   For our old black country.

   CHORUS

3. And if we have to die,
   What does it really matter? Our children
   Everywhere will be able to say how
   Triumph comes through battle,
   And in the smallest village
   Sing beneath our three colours.

   CHORUS

COSTA RICA

Words by
JOSÉ MARÍA ZELEDÓN BRENES (1877 - 1949)

Music by
MANUEL MARÍA GUTIÉRREZ (1829 - 1887)

No - ble pa - tria tu her - mo - sa ban - de - ra Ex - pre-
sión de tu vi - da nos da: Ba - jo el lím - pi - do a - zul de tu

The music was adopted in 1853; the words were chosen as a result of a public competition in 1900.

154

cie - lo Blan - ca y pu - ra des - can - sa la paz.

En la lu - cha te - naz de fe - cun - da la - bor Que en ro-

je - ce del hom - bre la faz, Con - qui - sta - ron tus

hi - jos, la - brie - gos sen - ci - llos, E - ter - no pres - ti - gio, es - ti - ma y ho-

nor, E - ter - no pres - ti - gio, es - ti - ma y ho - nor.

¡Sal - ve, oh tie - rra gen - til! ¡Sal - ve, oh ma - dre de a -

mor! Cuan-do al - gu - no pre - ten - da tu glo - ria man -

char,_____ Ve - rás a tu pue - blo, va - lien - te y vi -

ril, La____ tos - ca he - rra - mien - ta en ar - ma tro -

car. ¡Sal - ve, oh pa - tria! tu pró - di - go sue - lo Dul - ce a -

bri - go y sus - ten - to nos da; Ba - jo el lím - pi - do a-zul de tu

cie - lo ¡Vi - van siem - pre el tra - ba - jo y la paz!

ff

rall.

Translation by T. M. Cartledge

Noble homeland, your beautiful flag
Expresses for us your life:
Under the limpid blue of your skies,
Peace reigns, white and pure.
In the tenacious battle of fruitful toil,
That brings a glow to men's faces,
Your sons, simple farm hands,
Gained eternal renown, esteem and honour. } (twice)
Hail, gentle country!
Hail, loving mother!
If anyone should attempt to besmirch your glory,
You will see your people, valiant and virile,
Exchange their rustic tools for weapons.
Hail, O homeland! Your prodigal soil
Gives us sweet sustenance and shelter.
Under the limpid blue of your sky,
May peaceful labour ever continue.

CROATIA

Words by
ANTUN MIHANOVIĆ (1796 - 1861)

Music by
JOSIP RUNJANIN (1821 - 1878)
Arr. by W. L. REED

1. Lije - pa na - ša do - mo - vi - no, Oj ju - na - čka ze - mljo mi - la,

Sta - re sla - ve dje do - vi - no, Da bi va — zda sre - tna bi - la!

Mi - la, ka - no si nam — sla - vna, Mi - la si nam ti je - di - na.

Adopted on 22 December, 1990. Croatia achieved independence on 15 January, 1992.

Mi - la, ku - da si nam ra - vna, Mi - la, ku - da si pla - ni - na!

2. *Teci Dravo, Savo teci,*
   Nit' ti Dunav silu gubi,
   Sinje more svijetu reci,
   Da svoj narod Hrvat ljubi.
   Dok mu njive sunce grije,
   Dok mu hrašće bura vije,
   Dok mu mrtve grobak krije,
   Dok mu živo srce bije!

Translation

1. Our beautiful homeland,
   Oh dear, heroic land,
   Fatherland of ancient glory,
   May you always be happy!
   Dear, as much as you are glorious,
   Only you are dear to us.
   Dear, where your land is flat,
   Dear, where it is mountainous.

2. Flow Drava, Sava flow,
   Nor you, Danube, lose your power,
   Azure sea, tell to the world
   That a Croat loves his nation.
   As long as sun warms his ploughed land,
   As long as storms lash his oak trees,
   As long as the grave hides his dead,
   As long as his living heart beats!

CUBA
La Bayamesa
(The Bayamo Song)

Words and music by
PEDRO FIGUEREDO (1819 - 1870)

Sung for the first time in 1868 during the battle of Bayamo, in which Figueredo played a leading part.

me - ses, Que la Pa - tria os con - tem - pla or - gu-

llo - sa; No te - máis u - na muer - te glo - rio -

sa, Que mo - rir por la Pa - tria es vi - vir._____ En ca-

de - nas vi - vir, es vi - vir_____ En a-

Translation by T. M. Cartledge

Hasten to battle, men of Bayamo,
For the homeland looks proudly to you.
You do not fear a glorious death,
Because to die for the country is to live.
To live in chains
Is to live in dishonour and ignominy. } (twice)
Hear the clarion call,
Hasten, brave ones, to battle!

CYPRUS

Imnos eis tin Eleftherian
(Hymn to Freedom)

Words by
DIONYSIOS SOLOMÓS (1798 - 1857)

Music by
NIKOLAOS MANTZAROS (1795 - 1873)

Se - gno - ri - so a - po tin Kop - si tou spa-
thiou tin tro - me - ri;____ Se - gno - ri - so a - po tin
op - si pou me via me - tra tin yi.____ Ap ta

Adopted in 1960. The National Anthem of Cyprus is the same as that of Greece.

prot' an - thri - o - me - ni hai - re o hai - r'e - lef - the - ria.

English versification by T. M. Cartledge

I shall always recognise you
By the dreadful sword you hold,
As the earth, with searching vision,
You survey, with spirit bold.
'Twas the Greeks of old whose dying
Brought to birth our spirit free.
Now, with ancient valour rising,
Let us hail you, oh Liberty! } (three times)

CZECH REPUBLIC

Words by
JOSEF KAJETÁN TYL (1808 - 1856)

Music by
FRANTIŠEK JAN ŠKROUP (1801 - 1862)

1. Kde do-mov můj, kde do-mov můj? Vo-da hu-čí po lu-či-nách, bo-ry šu-mi po ska-li-nách, v sa-dě skvi se ja-ra květ, zem-ský

The State hymn of Czechoslovakia was composed in 1834, and officially recognised as the National Anthem in 1919. It was in two sections - Czech and Slovak. The Czech section has been retained by the new Czech Republic as the National Anthem. When Slovakia separated from the rest of the country on 1 January, 1993, she retained the Slovak section as her National Anthem.

Lyrics under the music:

ráj——— to na po - hled! A to je ta krá - sná ze - mě, ze - mě

če - ská, do - mov můj,— ze - mě če - ská, do - mov můj!

Translation

2. *Kde domov můj, kde domov můj?*
   V kraji znáš-li bohumilém,
   Duše útlé v tělě čilém,
   Mysl jasnou, znik a zdar,
   A tu sílu, vzdoru zmar.
   To je Čechů slavné plémě,
   Mezi Čechy domov můj,
   Mezi Čechy domuv můj.

1. Where is my home, where is my home?
   Water bubbles across the meadows,
   Pinewoods rustle among crags,
   The garden is glorious with spring blossom,
   Paradise on earth it is to see.
   And this is that beautiful land,
   The Czech land, my home,
   The Czech land, my home.

2. Where is my home, where is my home?
   If, in a heavenly land, you have met
   Tender souls in agile frames,
   Of clear mind, vigorous and prospering,
   And with a strength that frustrates all defiance,
   That is the glorious race of the Czechs,
   Among Czechs (is) my home,
   Among Czechs, my home.

DENMARK

Words by
ADAM GOTTLOB OEHLENSCHLÄGER (1779 - 1850)

Music by
HANS ERNST KRØYER (1798 - 1879)

Words written in 1820. Its popularity as a National Anthem dates from 4 July, 1844, when students sang it at a national festival meeting to a gathering of 12,000 Danes. There are twelve verses.

Denmark also has a Royal Anthem (adopted 1780) with words by Johannes Ewald (1743 - 1781) and music by Ditlev Ludvig Rogert (1742 - 1813).

2. *Der sad i fordums tid*
   De harnisk klædte kæmper,
   Udhvilede fra strid;
   Udhvilede fra strid;
   Så drog de frem til fjenders men,
   Nu hvile deres bene
   Bag højens bautasten.   } (twice)

3. *Det land endnu er skønt,*
   Thi blå sig søen bælter,
   Og løvet står så grønt;
   Og løvet står så grønt;
   Og ædle kvinder, skønne mø'r
   Og mænd og raske svende
   Bebo de danskes øer.   } (twice)

Translation by R. P. Keigwin

1. There is a lovely land
   That proudly spreads her beeches
   Beside the Baltic strand.
   Beside the Baltic strand.
   A land that curves in hill and dale,
   That men have named Old Denmark,
   And this is Freya's hall.   } (twice)

2. There sat that earlier day
   The heroes in their harness
   And rested from the fray;
   And rested from the fray;
   Then forth they went, the foe they downed,
   But now their bones are resting
   'Neath bauta-stone and mound.   } (twice)

3. And still that land is fair,
   So blue the seas that belt her,
   So green the woodland there;
   So green the woodland there;
   And noble women, comely girls
   And men and lads of mettle
   Dwell in the Danish isles.   } (twice)

DJIBOUTI

Words by
ADEN ELMI (*b.* 1950)

Music by
ABDI ROBLEH (*b.* 1945)
Arr. by W. L. REED

Officially adopted in 1977.

Hinjinne u sara kaca
Calankaan harraad iyo
Haydaar u mudateen.

Hir cagaarku qariyayiyo
Habkay samadu tahayoo
Xiddig dhi igleh hoorshoo
Caddaan lagu hadheeyaay.

Maxaa haybad kugu yaal.

Translation

Arise with strength! For we have raised our flag,
The flag which has cost us dear
With extremes of thirst and pain.

Our flag, whose colours are the everlasting green of the earth,
The blue of the sky, and white, the colour of peace;
And in the centre the red star of blood.

Oh flag of ours, what a glorious sight !

DOMINICA

Words by
WILFRED OSCAR MORGAN POND (1912 - 1985)

Music by
LEMUEL McPHERSON CHRISTIAN (1913 - 2000)

Tempo di marcia

1. Isle of beau - ty, isle of splen - dour,

Isle to all so sweet and fair, All must sure - ly

gaze in won - der At thy gifts so rich and

Originally adopted in 1967 on achieving Statehood, and again in 1978 when becoming independent.

rare. Ri - vers,_____ val - leys, hills and_____ moun - tains,

All these gifts we do ex - tol. Heal - thy_____ land, so

like all_____ foun - tains, Giv - ing_____ cheer that warms the soul.

2. Dominica, God hath blest thee
   With a clime benign and bright,
   Pastures green and flowers of beauty
   Filling all with pure delight,
   And a people strong and healthy,
   Full of godly, rev'rent fear.
   May we ever seek to praise Thee
   For these gifts so rich and rare.

3. Come ye forward, sons and daughters
   Of this gem beyond compare.
   Strive for honour, sons and daughters,
   Do the right, be firm, be fair.
   Toil with hearts and hands and voices.
   We must prosper! Sound the call,
   In which ev'ryone rejoices,
   "All for Each and Each for All."

DOMINICAN REPUBLIC

Words by
EMILIO PRUD'HOMME (1856 - 1932)

Music by
JOSÉ REYÉS (1835 - 1905)

1. *Quis - que - ya - nos va - lien - tes, al - ce - mos Nues-tro can - to_ con vi - va e - mo - ción, Y_ del

Composed in 1883. First sung as National Anthem in 1900. There are six verses.
* Quisqueya is the native name of the island of Santo Domingo.

176

mun - do a la faz os - ten - te - mos Nues-tro in-vic - to glo-rio-so pen-

dón.   ¡Sal - ve el pue - blo que,in tré - pi - do y fuer - te,   A la

gue - rra a mo - rir se lan - zó   Cuan-do en bé - li - co re - to de

muer - te   Sus ca - de - nas de es - cla - vo rom-

pió.

cresc.

dim.

p

f

2. Nin - gun pue - blo ser li - bre me-

pp

f

re - ce Si es es - cla - vo in do - len - te y ser - vil; Si en su

dim.

f

pe - cho la lla - ma no cre - ce Que tem-

dim.

f

Translation by T. M. Cartledge

1. Brave men of Quisqueya,
   Let us sing with strong feeling
   And let us show to the world
   Our invincible, glorious banner.
   Hail, O people who, strong and intrepid,
   Launched into war and went to death!
   Under a warlike menace of death,
   You broke your chains of slavery.

2. No country deserves to be free
   If it is an indolent and servile slave,
   If the call does not grow loud within it,
   Tempered by a virile heroism.
   But the brave and indomitable Quisqueya
   Will always hold its head high,
   For if it were a thousand times enslaved,
   It would a thousand times regain freedom.

ECUADOR

Words by
JUAN LEÓN MERA (1832 - 1894)

Music by
ANTONIO NEUMANE (1818 - 1871)

Officially recognised by a government decree on 23 November, 1948. It had been in use since 1865. There are six verses.

bo - sa; Y tu fren - te,__ tu fren - te ra - dio - sa Más que el

sol con - tem - pla - mos lu - cir,_____ Y tu fren - te, tu fren - te ra-

dio - sa Más que el sol con - tem - pla - mos lu-

cir.   Y tu cir.   Los pri-

me - ros los hi - jos del sue - lo Que so - ber - bio, el Pi - chin - cha de-

co - ra Te a - cla - ma - ron por siem - pre___ se - ño - ra Y ver-

tie - ron su san - gre por ti. Dios mi - ró y a - cep - tó el ho - lo-

ca - us - to Ye - sa san - gre fue ger - men fe -
cun - do De o - tros hé - roes que a - tó - ni - to el
mun - do Vió en tu tor - no a mi - lla - res sur -
gir. Dios mi - gir, a mi - lla - res sur-

cresc.

cresc.

f

1. p   2. f

p ff f

gir,   a mi - lla - res sur - gir.

Translation by T. M. Cartledge

CHORUS

O homeland, we greet you a thousand times!
Glory be to you, O homeland, glory be to you!
Your breast overflows with joy and peace,
And we see your radiant face shining
More brightly than the sun.

The worthy sons of the soil
Which Pichincha on high is adorning,
Always acclaimed you as sovereign lady
And shed their blood for you.
God observed and accepted the sacrifice,
And that blood was the prolific seed
Of other heroes whom the world in astonishment saw   } (twice)
Arising in thousands around you.

CHORUS

EGYPT

Words and music by
SAYED DARWISH (1892 - 1923)
Arr. by W. L. REED

Allegretto Maestoso (♩ = 96)

CHORUS

Bi - la - di Bi - la - di Bi - la - di La - ki

Hu - bbi Wa Fu - a - di Bi - la - di Bi-

la - di Bi - la - di La - ki Hu - bbi Wa Fu -

Adopted in 1979.

186

2. *Misr Inti Aghla Durra*
   Fawq Gabeen Ad-dahr Ghurra
   Ya Biladi 'Aishi Hurra
   Wa As 'Adi Raghm-al-adi.

   CHORUS

3. *Misr Awladik Kiram*
   Aufiya Yar'u-zimam
   Saufa Takhti Bil-maram
   Bittihadhim Wa-ittihadi.

   CHORUS

Translation

CHORUS
My homeland, my homeland, my homeland,
My love and my heart are for thee.
My homeland, my homeland, my homeland,
My love and my heart are for thee.

1. Egypt! O mother of all lands,
   My hope and my ambition,
   How can one count
   The blessings of the Nile for mankind?

CHORUS

2. Egypt! Most precious jewel,
   Shining on the brow of eternity!
   O my homeland, be for ever free,
   Safe from every foe!

CHORUS

3. Egypt! Noble are thy children,
   Loyal, and guardians of thy soil.
   In war and peace
   We give our lives for thy sake.

CHORUS

EL SALVADOR

Words by
JUAN JOSÉ CAÑAS (1826 - 1918)

Music by
JUAN ABERLE (1846 - 1930)

Written in 1879 and adopted in 1953.

de - mos la Pa - tria or - gu - llo - sos De hi - jos

su - yos po - der - nos lla - mar_____ Y ju -

re - mos la vi - da a - ni - mo - sos Sin des -

can - so a su bien con - sa - grar.

can - so a su bien__ con - sa - grar,

con - sa - grar,

con - sa - grar, con - sa -

grar, con - sa - grar.__

FINE

1. De la paz en la di - cha su-
pre - - ma Siem - pre no - ble_____ so - ñó El Sal - va-
dor._____ Fué ob - te - ner - la su e - ter - no pro-
ble - ma, Con - ser - var - la es su glo - ria ma-

yor.   Y con fé in-que - bran - ta - ble el ca-

mi - no_____ Del pro - gre - so se a-fa - na en se-

guir en se - guir Por lle - nar_____ su gran - dio - so des-

ti - no,_____ Con - quis - tar - se un fe - liz_____ por - ve-

tad!_____ es - cri - bió_____ li - ber -

56

D.C. al Fine

tad!_____ es - cri - bió_____ li - ber - tad!

D.C. al Fine

57

CHORUS
Saludemos la patria orgullosos
De hijos suyos podernos llamar;
Y juremos la vida animosos,
Sin descanso a su bien consagrar.

2. *Libertad es su dogma, es su guía,*
   Que mil veces logró defender;
   Y otras tantas de audaz tirania
   Rechazar el odioso poder.
   Dolorosa y sangrienta es su historia,
   Pero excelsa y brillante a la vez,
   Manantial de legitima gloria,
   Gran lección de espartana altivez.
   No desmaya su innata bravura:
   En cada hombre hay un héroe inmortal,
   Que sabrá mantenerse a la altura
   De su antiguo valor proverbial.

CHORUS

3. *Todos son abnegados y fieles*
   Al prestigio del bélico ardor,
   Con que siempre segaron laureles
   De la Patria salvando el honor.
   Respetar los derechos extraños
   Y apoyarse en la recta razón
   Es para ella, sin torpes amaños,
   La invariable, más firme ambición.
   Y en seguir esta línea se aferra,
   Dedicando su esfuerzo tenaz
   En hacer cruda guerra a la guerra;
   Su ventura se encuentra en la paz.

CHORUS

CHORUS

Let us salute the motherland,
Proud to be called her children.
To her well-being let us swear
Boldly and unceasingly to devote our lives. } (twice)

1. Of peace enjoyed in perfect happiness,
   El Salvador has always nobly dreamed.
   To achieve this has been her eternal proposition,
   To keep it, her greatest glory.
   With inviolable faith, she eagerly follows
   The way of progress
   In order to fulfil her high destiny
   And acheive a happy future.
   A stern barrier protects her
   Against the clash of vile disloyalty,
   Ever since the day when her lofty banner,
   In letters of blood, wrote "Freedom,"
   Wrote "Freedom," wrote "Freedom."

   CHORUS

2. Freedom is her dogma and her guide;
   A thousand times she has defended it,
   And as many times has she repelled
   The hateful power of atrocious tyranny.
   Her history has been bloody and sad,
   Yet at the same time sublime and brilliant,
   A source of legitimate glory
   And a great lesson in Spartan pride.
   Her innate bravery shall not waver:
   In every man there is an immortal hero
   Who knows how to maintain the level
   Of the proverbial valour of old.

   CHORUS

3. All are self-denying and faithful
   To the tradition of warlike ardour
   With which they have always reaped fame
   By saving the motherland's honour.
   To respect the rights of others
   And base her actions on right and justice
   Is for her, without infamous intrigue,
   The constant and most firm ambition.
   And in following this line she persists,
   Dedicating her tenacious efforts
   In giving hard battle for battle;
   Her happiness is found in peace.

   CHORUS

EQUATORIAL GUINEA

Words by
ATANASIO NDONGO MIYONO (1928 - 1969)

Music by
RAMIRO SANCHEZ LOPEZ *
Arr. by W. L. REED

Maestoso

Ca - mi - ne - mos pi - san - do las sen - das De nuestra in - men - sa fe - li - ci - dad. En fra - ter - ni - dad, sin se - pa - ra - ción,— ¡Can - te - mos Li - ber - tad! Tras dos

Adopted in 1968.
*Years of birth and death unknown.

den - cia na - cio - nal, Y con - ser - ve - mos, Y con - ser-

ve - mos La in - de - pen - den - cia na - cio - nal.

Translation by T. M. Cartledge

Let us tread the paths
Of our great happiness.
In brotherhood, undivided,
Let us sing for freedom!
Behind us are two centuries
Of colonial domination.
In brotherly unity, without discrimination,
Let us sing for freedom!
Let us shout: Long live Guinea!
Let us defend our freedom.
Always singing of our free Guinea,
Let us keep united.
Let us shout: Long live Guinea!
Let us defend our freedom.
Always singing of our free Guinea,
Let us keep our nation independent,
Let us keep our nation independent.

ERITREA

Words by
SOLOMON TSEHAYE BERAKI (*b.* 1956)

Music by
ISAAC ABRAHAM MEHAREZGI (*b.* 1944)
and ARON TEKLE TESFATSION (*b.* 1963)
Arr. by ELIAS W. GABRIEL G. MICHAEL

Adopted on 19 May, 1993.

ra,———————— Ab-a-lem che-bi-ta-to g-bué kb - ra.   3. Na - ts   ra.

Translation from Tigrinya by Elsa Gebreyesus & Solomon Tsehaye

1. Eritrea, Eritrea, Eritrea,
   Her sacrifices, rewarded by freedom,
   Brought on her enemy's doom.

2. Decades of tenacity for her cause –
   So that her name,
   Symbol of fortitude it became,
   Etitrea, pride of the downtrodden,
   That truth triumphs, she has proven.

   CHORUS
   Eritrea, Eritrea
   Achieve her honourable place
   Among the family of nations.

3. The high moral that won freedom
   Shall proceed for developing
   The next noble aim.
   We vow to crown her
   With glory and prosperity,
   And make her the land of plenty.

   CHORUS

ESTONIA

Words by
JOHANN VOLDEMAR JANNSEN (1819 - 1900)

Music by
FRIEDRICH PACIUS (1809 - 1891)
Arr. by HENRY COLEMAN

Sung publicly for the first time at the First Estonian National Song Festival in Tartu on 1 July, 1869. The melody though shorter is the same as that of the National Anthem of Finland.

mull'   nii ar - mas o - leks   ka   Kui sa mu i - sa - maa!

2. *Sa oled mind ju sünnitand*
   Ja üles kasvatand;
   Sind tänan mina alati
   Ja jään sul truuks surmani!
   Mul kõige armsam oled sa,
   Mu kallis isamaa!

3. *Su üle Jumal valvaku,*
   Mu armas isamaa!
   Ta olgu sinu kaitseja
   Ja võtku rohkest' õnnista'
   Mis iial ette võtad sa,
   Mu kallis isamaa!

Translation by Jenny Wahl

1. My native land, my joy, delight,
   How fair thou art and bright!
   And nowhere in the world all round
   Can ever such a place be found
   So well beloved as I love thee,
   My native country dear!

2. My little cradle stood on thy soil,
   Whose blessings ease my toil.
   With my last breath my thanks to thee,
   For true to death I'll ever be,
   O worthy, most beloved and fine,
   Thou, dearest country mine!

3. May God in Heaven thee defend,
   My best, my dearest land!
   May He be guard, may He be shield,
   For ever may He bless and wield
   O graciously all deeds of thine,
   Thou dearest country mine!

ETHIOPIA

Words by
DEREJE MELAKU MENGESHA (*b.* 1957)

Music by
SOLOMON LULU MITIKU (*b.* 1950)
Arr. by W. L. REED

Adopted in 1992.

Yäzêgennät Keber Bä-Ityopp'yachchen S'änto
Tayyä Hezbawinnät Dar Eskädar Bärto.
Läsälam Läfeteh Lähezboch Näs'annät;
Bä'ekkulennät Bäfeqer Qomänal Bä'andennät.
Mäsärätä S'enu Säbe'enan Yalsharen;
Hezboch Nän Läsera Bäsera Yänoren.
Denq Yäbahel Mädräk Yä'akuri Qers Baläbet;
Yätäfät'ro S'ägga Yäjägna Hezb Ennat.
Ennet'äbbeqeshallän Alläbben Adära;
Ityopp'yachchen nuri Eññam Banchi Ennekura!

Translation by D. L. Appleyard

Respect for citizenship is strong in our Ethiopia;
National pride is seen, shining from one side to another.
For peace, for justice, for the freedom of peoples,
In equality and in love we stand united.
Firm of foundation, we do not dismiss humanness;
We are peoples who live through work.
Wonderful is the stage of tradition, mistress of proud heritage,
Mother of natural virtue, mother of a valorous people.
We shall protect you - we have a duty;
Our Ethiopia, live! And let us be proud of you!

FIJI

Words by
MICHAEL FRANCIS
    ALEXANDER PRESCOTT (b. 1928) *

Music by
CHARLES AUSTIN MILES (1868 - 1946)
Adapted by
MICHAEL FRANCIS ALEXANDER PRESCOTT

It won first prize in a nationwide contest before Fiji became independent in 1970.
* Year of death unknown.

Fi - ji, for ev - er - more!_____

2. Blessing grant, oh God of nations, on the isles of Fiji,
   Shores of golden sand and sunshine, happiness and song.
   Stand united, we of Fiji, fame and glory ever,
   Onward march together, God bless Fiji!

   CHORUS

FINLAND

Original Swedish words by
JOHAN LUDVIG RUNEBERG (1804 - 1877)
Finnish words by
PAAVO EEMIL KAJANDER (1846 - 1913)

Music by
FREDRIK PACIUS (1809 - 1891)

The words were written in 1846. Sung for the first time at a student's gathering on 13 May, 1848. The melody is the same as that of the National Anthem of Estonia.

214

ko - ti - maa tää poh - joi - nen, Maa kal - lis i - si - en!

2. *Sun kukoistukses kuorestaan*
   Kerrankin puhkeaa!
   Viel' lempemme saa nousemaan
   Sun toivos, riemus loistossaan,
   Ja kerran laulus, synnyinmaa,
   Korkeemman kaiun saa!

Swedish	Translation by Charles Wharton Stork

1. *Vårt land, vårt land, vårt fosterland,*
   Ljud högt, o dyra ord!
   Ej lyfts en höjd mot himlens rand,
   Ej sänks en dal, ej sköljs en strand,
   Mer älskad än vår bygd i nord,
   Än våra fäders jord.

2. *Din blomning, sluten än i knopp,*
   Skall mogna ur sitt tvång;
   Se, ur vår kärlek skall gå opp
   Ditt ljus, din glans, din fröjd, ditt hopp,
   Och högra klinga skall en gång
   Vår fosterländska sång.

1. Our land, our land, our native land,
   Oh, let her name ring clear!
   No peaks against the heavens that stand,
   No gentle dales or foaming strand
   Are loved as we our home revere,
   The earth our sires held dear.

2. The flowers in their buds that grope
   Shall burst their sheaths with spring;
   So from our love to bloom shall ope
   Thy gleam, thy glow, thy joy, thy hope,
   And higher yet some day shall ring
   The patriot song we sing!

FRANCE
La Marseillaise

Words and music by
CLAUDE-JOSEPH ROUGET DE L'ISLE (1760 - 1836)

1. Al - lons en - fants de la Pa - tri - e, Le jour de gloire est ar - ri - vé. Con - tre nous, de la ty - ran - ni - e, L'é - ten - dard sang - lant est le - vé, l'e - ten-

Written and composed on 24 April, 1792, as a marching song. Adopted as the National Anthem on 15 July, 1795.
The National Anthem of France is also used in French Guiana, French Polynesia, Guadeloupe, Martinique, Mayotte, New Caledonia, Réunion, St. Pierre-Miquelon and Wallis & Futuna Islands.

* This part of the Anthem is generally repeated

2. *Amour sacré de la Patrie,*
   Conduis, soutiens nos bras vengeurs.
   Liberté, liberté chérie,
   Combats avec tes défenseurs; } (twice)
   Sous nos drapeaux, que la victoire
   Accoure à tes mâles accents;
   Que tes ennemis expirants
   Voient ton triomphe et notre glorie!
   Aux armes citoyens! etc.

Translation by T. M. Cartledge

1. Arise, children of the fatherland,
   The day of glory has come.
   Against us the blood-stained banner
   Of tyranny is raised,
   The banner of tyranny is raised,
   Hear, in the fields, the roar
   Of her fierce soldiers.
   They come right into our arms
   To slaughter our sons and our consorts.
   Patriots, to arms!
   Form your battalions,
   Let's march, let's march!
   May the tyrant's foul blood water our furrows!

2. Sacred love of country,
   May you guide and sustain our avenging hands.
   Freedom, dear freedom,
   Fight along with those who defend you,
   Fight along with those who defend you.
   Under our flags, may victory
   Follow your manly accents;
   May your dying enemies
   See your triumph and our glory!
   Patriots, to arms!
   Form your battalions,
   Let's march, let's march!
   May the tyrant's foul blood water our furrows!

GABON

Words and music by
GEORGES ALEKA DAMAS (1902 - 1982)
Arr. by HENRY COLEMAN

Adopted on 17 August, 1960.

l'in - jus - tice et la hon - te. Qu'il mon -

te, monte en - co - - - re et cal - me nos a -

lar - - - mes, Qu'il prô - ne la ver - tu

et re - pous - se les armes. U -

CHORUS
D. %

D. %

221

2. *Oui que le temps heureux rêvé par nos ancêtres*
   Arrive enfin chez nous, rejouisse les êtres,
   Et chasse les sorciers, ces perfides trompeurs
   Qui semaient le poison et répandaient la peur.

   CHORUS

3. *Afin qu'aux yeux du monde et des nations amies*
   Le Gabon immortel reste digne d'envie,
   Oublions nos querelles, ensemble bâtissons
   L'édifice nouveau auquel tous nous rêvons.

   CHORUS

4. *Des bords de l'Océan au cœur de la forêt,*
   Demeurons vigilants, sans faiblesse et sans haine!
   Autour de ce drapeau, qui vers l'honneur nous mène,
   Saluons la Patrie et chantons sans arrêt:

   CHORUS

Translation by T. M. Cartledge

CHORUS
United in concord and brotherhood,
Awake, Gabon, dawn is at hand.
Stir up the spirit that thrills and inspires us!
At last we rise up to attain happiness.

1. Dazzling and proud, the sublime day dawns,
   Dispelling for ever injustice and shame.
   May it still advance and calm our fears,
   May it promote virtue and banish warfare.

   CHORUS

2. Yes, may the happy days of which our ancestors dreamed
   Come for us at last, rejoicing our hearts,
   And banish the sorcerers, those perfidious deceivers
   Who sowed poison and spread fear.

   CHORUS

3. So that, in the eyes of the world and of friendly nations,
   The immortal Gabon may maintain her good repute,
   Let us forget our quarrels, let us build together
   The new structure of which we all have dreamed.

   CHORUS

4. From the shores of the Ocean to the heart of the forest,
   Let us remain vigilant, without weakness and without hatred!
   Around this flag which leads us to honour,
   Let us salute the Fatherland and ever sing:

   CHORUS

THE GAMBIA

Words by
VIRGINIA JULIE HOWE (*b*. 1927)

Composer unknown
Adapted by
JEREMY FREDERICK HOWE (*b*. 1929)*
Arr. by W. L. REED

For The Gam - bi - a, our— home - land, We— strive and work and pray, That— all may— live in u - ni - ty, Free - dom and peace each day. Let jus - tice guide our ac - tions To - wards the com - mon

Officially adopted on 18 February, 1965.
* The melody is a traditional Mandika song 'Foday Kaba Dumbuya'.

good, And— join our di - verse peo - ples To—

prove man's bro - ther - hood. We pledge our firm al -

le - giance, Our— pro - mise we re - new; Keep

us, great God of na - tions, To The Gam - bia ev - er true.

GEORGIA

Words by
DAWIT MAGRADSE *

Music by
ZAKARIA PALIASHVILA (1871 - 1933)
Adapted by JOSEB KETSCHAKMADSE

Adopted on 23 April, 2004.
* Dates not yet available.

Translation

<table>
<tr><td>

Chemi sat'ia samshoblo,
Sakhat'e mteli kveq'ana,
Ganatebuli mta-bari,
Ts'ilnaq'aria ghmerttana.
Tavisupleba dghes chveni
Momavals umghers didebas,
Tsisk'ris varsk'vslavi amodis
Da or zghvas shua brts'q'indeba,
Dideba tavisuplebas,
Tavisuplebas didebas!

</td><td>

My icon is my motherland,
Holiness is all the world,
Lightened mountains and valleys,
Is the gift from God.
Today's independence of ours,
Praising glory to the future.
Morning's star is rising
And sparkling between two seas.
Glory to Freedom,
Freedom to Glory.

</td></tr>
</table>

GERMANY

Words by
AUGUST HEINRICH HOFFMANN von FALLERSLEBEN (1798 - 1874)

Music by
FRANZ JOSEPH HAYDN (1732 - 1809)

Ein - ig - keit und Recht und Frei - heit Für das deut - sche Va - ter - land! Da - nach lasst uns al - le stre - ben Brü - der - lich mit Herz und Hand! Ein - ig -

Authorised on 11 August, 1922, when the first verse of Hoffmann von Fallersleben's poem was sung. In 1952 the Federal Republic adopted the three verses as the official words. The re-unification of West and East Germany took place on 3 October, 1990, when the National Anthem of West Germany was retained and the third verse only was officially adopted.

keit— und Recht und Frei - heit Sind des Glück - es Un - ter -

pfand. Blüh im Glan - ze die - ses

Glück - es, Blü - he,— deut - sches— Va - ter - land!

Translation

Unity and Right and Freedom
For the German Fatherland!
After these let us all strive
Brotherly with heart and hand!
Unity and Right and Freedom
Are the pledge of happiness.
Bloom in the splendour of this happiness,
Bloom, my German Fatherland! } (twice)

GHANA

Words by the
GHANA GOVERNMENT

Music by
PHILIP GBEHO (1905 - 1976)

Officially became the National Anthem in 1957, the year when independence was attained. The original words were written in 1956, as was the music, but replaced by the present text following a change of government in 1966.

- mil - i - ty, Make— us cher - ish— fear - less hon - es - ty,—

And help us to re - sist op - pres - sor's rule With all our

will and might— for ev - er - more.————— more.

2. Hail to thy name, O Ghana,
   To thee we make our solemn vow:
   Steadfast to build together
   A nation strong in Unity;
   With our gifts of mind and strength of arm,
   Whether night or day, in mist or storm,
   In ev'ry need, whate'er the call may be,
   To serve thee, Ghana, now and evermore. } (twice)

3. Raise high the flag of Ghana
   And one with Africa advance;
   Black Star of hope and honour
   To all who thirst for Liberty;
   Where the banner of Ghana freely flies,
   May the way to freedom truly lie;
   Arise, arise, O sons of Ghanaland,
   And under God march on for evermore! } (twice)

GIBRALTAR

Words and music by
PETER EMBERLEY (*b.* 1955)
Arr. by BARRIE HINGLEY and W. L. REED

Chosen as a result of a competition and officially adopted on 18 October, 1994.

Port of hope in times of need, rich in hist-o-ry. Gib-

ral - tar, Gib - ral - tar, the rock on which I stand,

May you be for - ev - er free, Gib - ral - tar, my own land.

God give grace to this our home-land, help us to live as one.

GREECE
Imnos Eis Tin Eleftherian
(Hymn To Freedom)

Words by
DIONYSIOS SOLOMÓS (1798 - 1857)

Music by
NIKOLAOS MANTZAROS (1795 - 1873)

Chosen by King George I and adopted in 1864. There are one hundred and fifty eight verses. The National Anthem of Greece is the same as that of Cyprus.

235

prot' an - thri - o - me - ni hai - re o hai - r'e - lef - the - ria.___

English versification by T. M. Cartledge

I shall always recognise you
By the dreadful sword you hold,
As the earth, with searching vision,
You survey, with spirit bold.
'Twas the Greeks of old whose dying
Brought to birth our spirit free.
Now, with ancient valour rising,
Let us hail you, oh Liberty! } (three times)

GRENADA

Words by
IRVA MERLE BAPTISTE-BLACKETT (*b.* 1924)

Music by
LOUIS ARNOLD MASANTO (*b.* 1938)

Hail! Gre - na - da, land of ours, We pledge our - selves to thee, Heads, hearts— and— hands in u - ni - ty To

Officially adopted on 7 February, 1974.

reach our des - ti - ny. Ev - er con - scious of God, Be - ing

proud of our her - it - age, May we with faith and

cour - age As - pire,——— build, ad - vance As one

peo - ple, one fam - i - ly. God bless our na - tion.

GUATEMALA

Words by
JOSÉ JOAQUÍN PALMA (1844 - 1911)

Music by
RAFAEL ALVAREZ OVALLE (1860 - 1948)

Chosen from entries in a public competition in 1887. Adopted by governmental decrees of 28 October, 1896 and 19 February, 1897, and modified by decree of 26 July, 1934. There are four verses.

fie - ra An - tes muer - to q'es - cla - vo se - rá.

36

Translation by T. M. Cartledge

VERSE
Fortunate Guatemala! May your altars
Never be profaned by cruel men.
May there never be slaves who submit to their yoke,
Or tyrants who deride you.
If tomorrow your sacred soil
Should be threatened by foreign invasion,
Your fair flag, flying freely in the wind,
Will call to you: Conquer or die.

CHORUS
Your fair flag, flying freely in the wind,
Will call to you: Conquer or die;
For your people, with heart and soul,
Would prefer death to slavery.

GUINEA
Liberté

Author unknown

Music by
FODEBA KEITA (1922 - 1969)

Adopted in 1958.

Peuple d'Afrique!
Le Passé historique!
Que chante l'hymne de la Guinée fière et jeune -
Illustre epopée de nos frères
Morts au champ d'honneur en libérant l'Afrique!
Le peuple de Guinée prêchant l'unité
Appelle l'Afrique.
Liberté! C'est la voix d'un peuple
Qui appelle tous ses frères a se retrouver.
Liberté! C'est la voix d'un peuple
Qui appelle tous ses frères de la grande Afrique.
Bâtissons l'unité africaine dans l'indépendance retrouvée.

Translation

People of Africa!
The historic past!
Sing the hymn of a Guinea proud and young -
Illustrious epic of our brothers
Who died on the field of honour while liberating Africa!
The people of Guinea, preaching Unity,
Call to Africa.
Liberty! The voice of a people
Who call all her brothers to find their way again.
Liberty! The voice of a people
Who call all her brothers of a great Africa.
Let us build African Unity in a newly found independence!

GUINEA-BISSAU
É Pátria Amada
(Our Beloved Fatherland)

Words and music by
AMILCAR LOPES CABRAL (1924 - 1973)

Allegro moderato, alla marcia

1. Sol, su - or e o ver - de e mar,

Sé - cu - los de dor e es - peran - ça: Es - ta é a ter - ra dos

Composed in 1963. Adopted on Independence Day, 24 September, 1974.

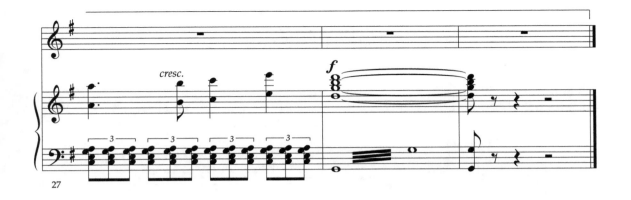

27

2. *Ramos do mesmo tronco,*
   Olhos na mesma luz:
   Esta é a força da nossa união!
   Cantem o mar e a terra
   A madrugada eo sol
   Que a nossa luta fecundou.

   CHORUS

Translation

1. Sun, sweat, verdure and sea,
   Centuries of pain and hope;
   This is the land of our ancestors.
   Fruit of our hands,
   Of the flower of our blood:
   This is our beloved country.

   CHORUS
   Long live our glorious country!
   The banner of our struggle
   Has fluttered in the skies.
   Forward, against the foreign yoke!
   We are going to build
   Peace and progress
   In our immortal country! } (twice)

2. Branches of the same trunk,
   Eyes in the same light;
   This is the force of our unity!
   The sea and the land,
   The dawn and the sun are singing
   That our struggle has borne fruit!

   CHORUS

GUYANA

Words by
ARCHIBALD LEONARD LUKER (1917 - 1971)

Music by
ROBERT CYRIL GLADSTONE POTTER (1899 - 1981)
Arr. by W. L. REED

1. Dear land of Guy-a-na, of ri-vers and plains; Made rich by the sun-shine and lush by the rains, Set gem-like and fair be-tween moun-tains and sea, Your

The words and music were selected as the result of a competition, and were approved by the House of Assembly on 21 April, 1966. Guyana became independent on 26 May, 1966.

child - ren sa - lute you, dear land of the free.

2. Green land of Guyana, our heroes of yore,
   Both bondsmen and free, laid their bones on your shore.
   This soil so they hallowed, and from them are we,
   All sons of one Mother, Guyana the free.

3. Great land of Guyana, diverse through our strains,
   We are born of their sacrifice, heirs of their pains,
   And ours is the glory their eyes did not see -
   One land of six peoples, united and free.

4. Dear land of Guyana, to you will we give
   Our homage, our service, each day that we live;
   God guard you, great Mother, and make us to be
   More worthy our heritage - land of the free.

HAITI
La Dessalinienne
(The Dessalines Song)

Words by
JUSTIN LHÉRISSON (1873 - 1907)

Music by
NICOLAS GEFFRARD (1871 - 1930)

1. Pour le Pa - ys, Pour la Pa - tri - e, Mar - chons u - nis, Mar - chons u - nis. Dans nos rangs point de traî - tres! Du sol soy - ons seuls maî - tres. Pour le Pa -

Composed for the centenary of national independence in 1904. The title is derived from Jean-Jacques Dessalines, the founder of Haiti as an independent republic.

ys, Pour la Pa - tri - e Mar - chons u - nis, Mar - chons u -

nis. Mar - chons, mar - chons mar - chons u - nis, Pour le Pa -

ys, Pour la Pa - tri - e.

2. *Pour les Aïeux,*
   Pour la Patrie
   Bêchons joyeux:
   Quand le champ fructifie
   L'âme se fortifie.
   Bêchons joyeux
   Pour les Aïeux,
   Pour la Patrie.

3. *Pour le Pays*
   Et pour nos Pères
   Formons des Fils.
   Libres, forts et prospères,
   Toujours: nous serons frères,
   Formons des fils
   Pour le Pays
   Et pour nos Pères.

4. *Pour les Aïeux,*
   Pour la Patrie
   O Dieu des Preux!
   Sous ta garde infinie
   Prends nos droits, notre vie,
   O Dieu des Preux!
   Pour les Aïeux,
   Pour la Patrie.

5. *Pour le Drapeau,*
   Pour la Patrie
   Mourir est beau!
   Notre passé nous crie:
   Ayez l'âme aguerrie!
   Mourir est beau
   Pour le Drapeau,
   Pour la Patrie.

Translation by T. M. Cartledge

1. For our country,
   For our forefathers,
   United let us march.
   Let there be no traitors in our ranks!
   Let us be masters of our soil.
   United let us march
   For our country,
   For our forefathers.

2. For our forebears,
   For our country
   Let us toil joyfully.
   May the fields be fertile
   And our souls take courage.
   Let us toil joyfully
   For our forebears,
   For our country.

3. For our country
   And for our forefathers,
   Let us train our sons.
   Free, strong and prosperous,
   We shall always be as brothers.
   Let us train our sons
   For our country
   And for our forefathers.

4. For our forebears,
   For our country,
   Oh God of the valiant!
   Take our rights and our life
   Under your infinite protection,
   Oh God of the valiant!
   For our forebears,
   For our country.

5. For the flag,
   For our country
   To die is a fine thing!
   Our past cries out to us:
   Have a disciplined soul!
   To die is a fine thing,
   For the flag,
   For our country.

Creole words by Raymond A. Moïse

1. *Pou Ayiti, peyi zansèt yo,*
   Se pou n' mache men nan lamen.
   Nan mitan n', pa fèt pou gen trèt,
   Nou fèt pou n' sèl mèt tèt nou.
   An nou mache men nan lamen
   Pou Ayiti ka vin bi bèl .
   An nou, an nou met tèt ansanm
   Pou Ayiti, onon tout zansèt yo.

2. *Pou Ayiti, onon zansèt yo,*
   Se pou n' sekle, se pou n' plante,
   Se nan tè tout fòs nou chita
   Se li k' ban nou manje.
   Ann bite tè, ann voye wou
   Ak kè kontan, fòk tè a bay.
   Sekle, wouze, fanm kou gason
   Pou n' rive viv ak sèl fòs ponyèt nou.

3. *Pou Ayiti, ak pou zansèt yo,*
   Fò nou kapab vanyan gason.
   Moun pa fèt pou ret avèk moun
   Se sa k' fè tout manman ak tout papa
   Dwe pou voye timoun lekòl
   Pou yo aprann, pou yo konnen
   Sa Tousen, Desalin, Kristòf, Petyon
   Te fè pou wet Ayisyen anba kòf blan.

4. *Pou Ayiti, onon zansèt yo,*
   Ann leve tèt nou gad anlè,
   Pou tout moun mande Granmèt la
   Pou l' ba nou pwoteksyon.
   Pou move zanj pa detounen n'
   Pou n' ka mache nan bon chimen
   Pou libète ka libète,
   Fòk lajistis blayi sou peyi a.

5. *Nou gen on drapo tankou tout pèp.*
   Se pou n' renmen l', mouri pou li,
   Se pa kado blan te fè nou
   Se san zansèt nou yo ki te koule
   Pou nou kenbe drapo nou wo,
   Se pou n' travay, met tèt ansanm
   Pou lòt peyi ka respekte l'
   Drapo sila a se nanm tout Ayisyen.

HONDURAS

Words by
AUGUSTO CONSTANCIO COELLO (1883 - 1941)

Music by
CARLOS HARTLING (1869 - 1920)

Tu ban-de-ra, tu ban-de-ra Es un lam-po de cie-lo Por un blo-que, por un blo-que De nie-ve cru-za-do; Y se

Selected as a result of a public competition, and adopted in 1915. There are six verses.

lah ta - nah - ku, Hi - dup - lah ne - gri-ku, Bang - sa - ku, Rak - jat-ku se - 'm-

wa — nja. Ba - ngun - lah ji - wa-nja, Ba - ngun - lah ba - dan - nja Un - tuk

CHORUS

ff

In - do - ne - sia Ra - ja. In - do - ne - sia Ra - ja, Mer - de-

ka, Mer - de - ka, Ta - nah-ku ne - gri-ku jang ku-tjin - ta. In - do-

ne - sia Ra-ja, Mer - de - ka, Mer - de - ka, Hi - dup-

molto ritard. 2nd time

1.

2.

lah In - do-ne - sia Ra - ja. In - do - ja.

molto ritard. 2nd time

2. *Indonesia! Tanah jang mulia,*
   Tanah kita jang kaja.
   Disanalah aku berada
   Untuk s'lamalamanja.
   Indonesia Tanah pusaka,
   P'saka Kita semuanja.
   Marilah kita mendo'a,
   "Indonesia bahagia!"
   Suburlah Tanahnja,
   Suburlah jiwanja,
   Bangsanja, Rakjatnja se'mwanja.
   Sadarlah hatinja,
   Sadarlah budinja
   Untuk Indonesia Raja.

   CHORUS

3. *Indonesia! Tanah jang sutji,*
   Tanah kita jang sakti.
   Disanalah aku berdiri
   'Ndjaga ibu sedjati.
   Indonesia Tanah berseri,
   Tanah jang aku sajangi.
   Mirilah kita berdjandji,
   "Indonesia abadi!"
   S'lamatlah Rakjatnja,
   S'lamatlah putranja,
   Pulaunja, lautnja se'mwanja.
   Madjulah Negrinja,
   Madjulah Pandunja
   Untuk Indonesia Raja.

   CHORUS

Translation

1. Indonesia, our native country,
   Our birthplace,
   Where we all arise to stand guard
   Over this our Motherland:
   Indonesia our nationality,
   Our people and our country.
   Come then, let us all exclaim
   Indonesia united.
   Long live our land,
   Long live our state,
   Our nation, our people, and all
   Arise then, its spirit,
   Arise, its bodies
   For Great Indonesia.

   CHORUS
   Indonesia the Great, independent and free,
   Our beloved country.
   Indonesia the Great, independent and free,
   Long live Indonesia the Great!

2. Indonesia, an eminent country,
   Our wealthy country,
   There we shall be forever.
   Indonesia, the country of our
       ancestors,
   A relic of all of us.
   Let us pray
   For Indonesia's prosperity:
   May her soil be fertile
   And spirited her soul,
   The nation and all the people.
   Conscious be her heart
   And her mind
   For Indonesia the Great.

   CHORUS

3. Indonesia, a sacred country,
   Our victorious country:
   There we stand
   Guarding our true Mother.
   Indonesia, a beaming Country,
   A country we love with all our heart,
   Let's make a vow
   That Indonesia be there forever.
   Blessed be her people
   And her sons,
   All her islands, and her seas.
   Fast be the country's progress
   And the progress of her youth
   For Indonesia the Great.

   CHORUS

IRAN

Words written collectively

Music by
HASSAN RIAHI (b. 1945)
Arr. by W. L. REED

Andante con moto (♩ = 76)

Chosen as a result of a competition held in 1990.

Sar Zad Az Ufuq Mihr-i Ḫāwarān
Furūg-i Dīda-yi Ḥaqq-bāwarān
Bahman - Farr-i Īman-i Māst
Payāmat Ay Imām Istiqlāl. Azādī-naqš-i Ġan-i Māst
Sahīdān - Pīčīda Dar Gūš-i Zamān Faryād-i Tān
Pāyanda Mānī Wa Ġawidān
Gumhūrī-yi Islāmī-i Irān

Translation by W. L. Reed (from the German)

Upwards on the horizon rises the Eastern Sun,
The sight of the true Religion.
Bahman - the brilliance of our Faith.
Your message, O Imam, of independence and freedom
        is imprinted on our souls.
O Martyrs! The time of your cries of pain rings in our ears.
Enduring, continuing, eternal,
The Islamic Republic of Iran.

IRAQ

No words

Music by
LEWIS ZANBAKA (*b.* 1929)

This National Anthem was originally adopted in 1959, replaced in 1965, restored in 2003 and replaced in 2004. The current National Anthem adopted in 2004 has been unobtainable and is expected to be further replaced soon.

IRISH REPUBLIC
Amhrán na bhFiann
(The Soldier's Song)

Celtic words by
LIAM O'RINN (1888 - 1950)
English words by
PEADAR KEARNEY (1883 - 1942)

Music by
PATRICK HEENEY (1881 - 1911)
Arr. by T. M. CARTLEDGE

Sin - ne Fian - na Fáil, a - tá faoi gheall ag Éi - rinn,
Sol - diers are we, whose lives are pledged to Ire - land;

Buíon dár slua thar toinn do rái - nig chughainn,
Some have come from a land be - yond the wave,

Faoi mhóid bheith saor, Sean - tir ár sin - sear
Sworn to be free, no more our an - cient

There were originally three verses and a chorus. The latter was adopted as the National Anthem in July 1926.

feas - ta Ní fhág - far faoin tior - án ná faoin
sire - land Shall shel - ter the des - pot or the

tráill. A - nocht a thé - am sa___ bhear - na baoil, Le
slave. To - night we man___ the___ bear - na baoil,* In

gean ar Ghaeil chun báis nó saoil, Le gun - na - scréach, faoi
Er - in's cause, come woe or weal, 'Mid can - non's___ roar and

lámhach na___ bpiléar, Seo libh can - aig amh - rán na bhFiann.
ri - fles___ peal, We'll___ chant___ a sol - dier's song.

* Pronounced 'Barna Bwail'. It means 'gap of danger'.

281

ISLE OF MAN

Words by
WILLIAM HENRY GILL (1839 - 1923)
Manx translation by
JOHN J. KNEEN (1873 - 1939)

Music adapted by
WILLIAM HENRY GILL (1839 - 1923)
From a Traditional Manx Air
Arr. by W. L. REED

There are eight verses in all. We give the first and last verses, which are those usually sung. W.H. Gill, a keen Manxman, was a collector and arranger of Manx music, of which he made a special study. J.J. Kneen was an expert on the Manx language and author of several books on it. For his scholarship he was awarded the Royal Norwegian Order of St. Olav by H.M. King Haakon VII in 1933, in recognition also of the historical connection between Norway and the Isle of Man.

fair;   Built——— firm   as   Bar - rool,
fide;   That——— each   sin - gle   hour
Yee,   Ta   dt'   Ard - stoyl   Reill - Thie
Chiarn;   Dy——— vod - mayd   dagh   oor,

Thy——— Throne   of   Home   Rule   Make   us
We——— trust   in   His   power,   No———
Myr——— Bar - rool   er   py hoie   Dy———
Treish——— teil   er   e   phooar,   Dagh———

10 a

free   as——— thy——— sweet moun - tain   air.———
e - vil——— our——— souls   can   be - tide.———
reayl   shin——— ayns——— seyr - snys   as   shee.———
olk   ass——— nyn——— an - mee - nyn   'hayrn.———

13

283

ISRAEL
Hatikvah
(The Hope)

Words by
NAFTALI HERZ IMBER (1856 - 1909)

Music by
SHMUEL COHEN (1870 - 1940)

Kol— od ba-le-vav pe-ni-mah Ne-fesh ye-hu-di ho-mi-yah, Ul-fa-a-tei— miz-rach ka-di-mah A-yin le-zi-on zo-fi-yah. Od lo av-dah tik-va-te-nu Ha-tik-vah bat

Adopted in 1948.

284

Translation

While yet within the heart - inwardly
The soul of the Jew yearns,
And towards the vistas of the East-eastwards
An eye to Zion looks.
'Tis not yet lost, our hope,
The hope of two thousand years,
To be a free people in our land
In the land of Zion and Jerusalem. } (twice)

ITALY
Inno di Mameli
(Mameli Hymn)

Words by
GOFFREDO MAMELI (1827 - 1849)

Music by
MICHELE NOVARO (1822 - 1885)

Fra -

Adopted on 2 June, 1946, on the establishment of the Republic. There are six verses in all.

tel - li   d'I - ta - lia,   l'I - ta - lia   s'è
des - ta,   Del - l'el - mo   di   Sci - pio   s'è
cin - ta   la   tes - ta.   Do - v'è   la   vit -
to - ria?   Le   por - ga   la   chio - ma,   Chè schia - va   di

cresc.   *rall.*   **f** *a tempo*

Ro - ma Id - di - o la____ cre - ò.

Allegro mosso

Fra - tel - li d'I - ta - lia, l'I - ta - lia s'è

des - ta, Dell 'el - mo di Sci - pio s'è cin - ta la tes - ta. Dov' - è la vit-

to - ria? Le por - ga la chio - ma, Chè schia - va di Ro - ma Id - dio la cre-

ven en su fon - do sa - gra - do Cin - co es - tre - llas de pá - li - do a-

cresc.

zul; En tu em - ble - ma que un mar ru - mo - ro - so Con sus

cresc.

on - das bra - ví - as es - cu - da, De un vol - cán, de un vol-

ff

cán Tras la ci - ma des - nu - da Hay un

258

lló;   Y al mi - rar   tu be-lle-za ex-ta-si - a - do   Al in -

flu - jo i-de-al de tu en-can - to,   La   or - la   a -

zul   de tu es - plén - di - do____   man - to   Con su

be   -   so de a - mor   con - sa - gró.

D.C. (al Fine after Verse 2)

D.C. (al Fine after Verse 2)

259

2. *Por guardar ese emblema divino,*
   Marcharemos Oh Patria a la muerte,
   Generosa será nuestra suerte,
   Si morimos pensando en tu amor.
   Defendiendo tu santa bandera
   Y en tus pliegues gloriosos cubiertos,
   Serán muchos, Oh Honduras tus muertos,
   Pero todos caerán con honor.

CHORUS

Translation by T. M. Cartledge

CHORUS
Your flag is a splendour of sky
Crossed with a band of snow;
And there can be seen, in its sacred depths,
Five pale blue stars.
In your emblem, which a rough sea
With its wild waves protects,
Behind the bare summit of a volcano,
A star brightly shines.

1. Like an Indian maiden you were sleeping,
   Lulled by the resonant song of your seas,
   When, set in your golden valleys,
   The bold navigator found you;
   And on seeing, enraptured, your beauty,
   And feeling your enchantment,
   He dedicated a kiss of love to the blue hem
   Of your splendid mantle.

CHORUS

2. To guard this sacred emblem
   We shall march, oh fatherland, to our death;
   Our death will be honoured
   If we die thinking of your love.
   Having defended your holy flag,
   And shrouded in its glorious folds,
   Many, Honduras, shall die for you,
   But all shall fall in honour.

CHORUS

HUNGARY

Words by
FERENC KÖLCSEY (1790 - 1838)

Music by
FERENC ERKEL (1810 - 1893)

Officially adopted in 1844. There are eight verses.

Nyújts fe - lé - je vé - dö kart, Ha küzd el - len -

ség - gel; Bal - sors a - kit ré - gen tép,

Hozz re - á vig esz - ten - döt, Meg - bün - höd - te

már e nép A múl - tat sjö - ven - döt.

Translation

God bless the Hungarians
With good cheer and prosperity.
Extend a protective arm
If they fight the enemy.
Torn by misfortune for long,
Give them happy years.
These people have expiated
The past and the future.

ICELAND
Lofsöngur
(Song of Praise)

Words by
MATTHÍAS JOCHUMSSON (1835 - 1920)

Music by
SVEINBJÖRN SVEINBJÖRNSSON (1847 - 1926)
Arr. by W. L. REED

Ó, guð, vors lands, ó, lands vors guð, vjer lof - um þitt heil - ag - a,
heil - ag - a nafn. Úr sól - kerf - um himn - ann - a knýt - a þjer kranz þín - ir
her - skar - ar, tím - ann - a safn. Fyr - ir þjer er einn dag - ur sem

Written and composed in 1874, when Iceland secured its own constitution and also celebrated the one thousandth anniversary of the first permanent Norwegian settlers. There are three verses.

Translation by Nicholas Jones

O God of our land, O our land's God,
We worship Thy holy, holy name.
From the solar systems of the heavens bind for you a wreath
Your warriors, the assembly of the ages.
For Thee is one day as a thousand years,
And a thousand years a day and no more,
One small flower of eternity with a quivering tear,
That prays to its God and dies.
Iceland's thousand years, Iceland's thousand years,
One small flower of eternity with a quivering tear,
That prays to its God and dies.

INDIA

Words and music by
RABINDRANATH TAGORE (1861 - 1941) *
Arr. by BRYSON GERRARD

First published 1912. Officially adopted by the Constitutional Assembly on 24 January, 1950, two days before the proclamation of the Republic. There are five verses in all. Only the first is usually sung.

*Rabindranath Tagore also wrote the words and music of the National Anthem of Bangladesh.

268

Jai - nă, Pā - ra - si - kă, Mu - sal - mā - nă, Kri - shtā - nī

Pū - ra - vă pash - chi - mă ā - sé ta - vă sim - hā - sa - nă -

pā - sé prē - mă - hā - ră ha - ya găn - thā.

Ja - nă - ga - nă - ai - kyă vi - dhā - ya - kă ja - yă hé! Bhā - ra - tă bhāg - yă vi -

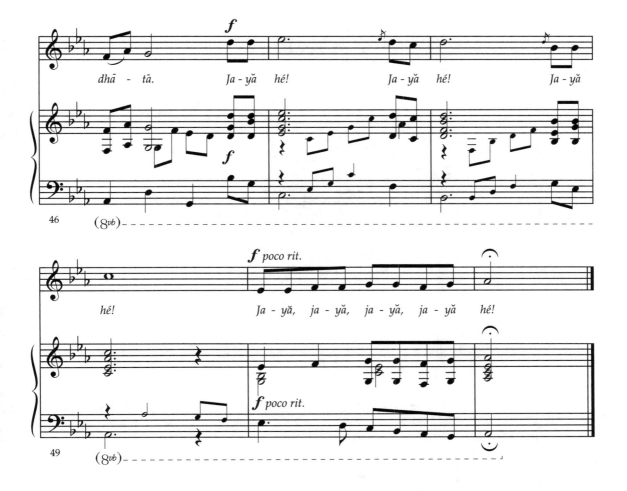

Translation

1. Glory to thee, ruler of our hearts and of India's destiny!
   Punjab, Sind, Gujrat, Maharashtra,
   The land of the Dravids, Orissa, Bengal,
   The Vindhyas and Himalayas, the Jamuna
   And the Ganges and the ceaseless waves of the Ocean
   All arise at thy fair name and seek thy blessings,
   Singing their hymn of praise to thee.
   Glory to thee, Oh Goddess of India's fortune!
   Hail, hail, hail to thee for ever!

2. Day and night thy call spreads over the land
   And we hear thy voice of salvation,
   Hindus, Buddhists, Sikhs, Jains,
   Parsees, Muslims and Christians
   Come from East and West to the foot of thy throne,
   Singing their song of devotion to thee.
   Oh glory to thee, who unites our hearts and gives us good fortune!
   Hail, hail, hail to thee for ever!

INDONESIA

Words and music by
WAGE RUDOLF SOEPRATMAN (1903 - 1938)

Adopted as the Nationalist Party Song in 1928, and became the National Anthem in 1949.

Translation

Italian Brothers,
Italy has awakened,
She has wreathed her head
With the helmet of Scipio.
Where is Victory?
She bows her head to you,
You, whom God created
As the slave of Rome.   (Repeat)
Let us band together,
We are ready to die,   } (twice)
Italy has called us.

IVORY COAST / CÔTE D'IVOIRE

L'Abidjanaise
(Song of Abidjan)

Words by
MATHIEU EKRA (*b.* 1917)
in collaboration with JOACHIM BONY (*b.* 1927)
and PIERRE MARIE COTY (*b.* 1927)

Music by
PIERRE MICHEL PANGO (*b.* 1926)
Arr. by M. J. BRISTOW

Salut ô ter - re d'es - pé - ran - ce;
Tes fils__ chè - re Côte d'I - voi - re

Pa - ys de l'hos - pi - ta - li - té.__ Tes lé - gions rem - plies de vail -
Fiers ar - ti - sans de ta gran - deur,__ Tous ras - sem - blés et pour ta

lan - ce Ont re - le - vé ta di - gni - té.__
gloi - re Te bâ - ti - ront dans le bon -

Adopted on 7 August, 1960.

heur. _____ Fiers I - voi - riens, le pa - ys nous ap -

pel - le. Si nous a - vons dans la paix ra - me -

né la li - ber - té, No - tre de - voir se - ra d'être

un mo - dè - le De l'es - pé - ran - ce ___ pro - mise

Translation by Elizabeth P. Coleman

We salute you, O land of hope,
Country of hospitality;
Thy gallant legions
Have restored thy dignity.
Beloved Ivory Coast, thy sons,
Proud builders of thy greatness,
All mustered together for thy glory,
In joy will construct thee.
Proud citizens of the Ivory Coast, the country calls us.
If we have brought back liberty peacefully,
It will be our duty to be an example
Of the hope promised to humanity,
Forging unitedly in new faith
The Fatherland of true brotherhood.

JAMAICA
Jamaica, Land We Love

Words by
HUGH BRAHAM SHERLOCK (1905 - 1998)

Music by
ROBERT CHARLES LIGHTBOURNE (1909 - 1995) *
Arr. by MAPLETOFT POULLE *

1. Eternal Father, bless our land, Guard us with Thy Mighty Hand, Keep us free from evil powers, Be our light through countless hours. To our Leaders, Great Defender,

Officially selected by the House of Representatives on 19 July, 1962.

* Mapletoft Poulle (1923 - 1981) blended the music (submitted separately to the National Anthem Committee) with the words (also submitted separately) to create the National Anthem.

Grant true wis-dom from— a - bove. Just - ice, Truth, be

ours for - ev - er, Ja - mai - ca, land we love. Ja-

mai - ca, Ja - mai - ca, Ja - mai - ca, land we love.

2. Teach us true respect for all,
   Stir response to duty's call,
   Strengthen us the weak to cherish,
   Give us vision lest we perish.
   Knowledge send us, Heavenly Father,
   Grant true wisdom from above.

   CHORUS

JAPAN
Kimigayo

Author unknown *

Music by
HIROMORI HAYASHI (1831 - 1896)
Arr. by W. L. REED

Ki - mi - ga— yo— wa Chi - yo - ni—— Ya - chi - yo - ni Sa - za - ré - i - shi no, I - wa - o to na - ri - té, Ko - ké no mu - su—— ma - dé.

Translation by Sazuko Takada

May thy peaceful reign last long!
May it last for thousands of years,
Until this tiny stone will grow into a massive rock
And the moss will cover it all deep and thick.

* Words selected from the seventh volume of *Kokinshu* dating from the 9th century.
First performed on 3 November, 1880, on Emperor Meiji's birthday, and approved on 12 August, 1893.

JORDAN

Words by
ABDUL-MONE'M AL-RIFAI' (1917 - 1985)

Music by
ABDUL-QADER AL-TANEER (1901 - 1957)

Largo ma non troppo

'A - sha al Ma - leek Sa - mi - yan Ma - qa - mu - hu

Kha - fi - qa - tin___ Fil Ma - 'a - li___ A - 'lam - u - hu.

Translation

Long live the King!
Long live the King!
His position is sublime,
His banners waving in glory supreme.

Adopted on 25 May, 1946.

296

KAZAKHSTAN

Words by
MUZAFAR ALIMBAYEV (*b.* 1923)

Music by
MUKAN TULEBAYEV (1913 - 1960)
and YEVGENY BRUSILOVSKY (1905 - 1981)

This National Anthem was adopted in 1992 and replaced in 2006. It has not been possible to obtain the replacement National Anthem in time for the 11th Edition.

1. *Azatyk zholinda zhalyndap zhanypyz*
   Tagdyrdin tezinen, tozaktyn ozinen
   Aman-sau kalyppyz, aman-sau kalyppyz.

   CHORUS
   Erkindik kyrany, sharykta
   Eldikke shakyryp tirlikte!
   Alyptyn kuaty - khalykta,
   Khalyktyn kuaty - birlikte!

2. *Ardaktan anasyn, kyrmetten danasyn,*
   Bauyrga baskanbyz barshanyn balasyn.
   Tatulyk dostyktyn kieli besigi!
   Meyirban Uly Otan, Kazakhtyn dalasy!

   CHORUS

3. *Talaydy otkerdin, otkenge salauat,*
   Keleshek gazhayyp keleshek galamat!
   Ar-ozhdan, ana til onege-saltymyz,
   Erlik te, eldik te urlakka amanat!

   CHORUS

Translation

1. We are brave people, children of honesty.
   We sacrificed all on the way to liberty.
   We have survived the kicks of fortune,
   Hell's fire, and came off unhurt.

   CHORUS
   Fly high the eagle of freedom,
   Calling for unity!
   People have the power of the hero,
   And the power of people is in unity.

2. Respecting mothers and the genius of the people,
   In the evil times we were open to everybody.
   Kazakh steppe is our motherland,
   The holy cradle of friendship and solidarity.

   CHORUS

3. Let the past teach us a lesson,
   We believe in a bright future.
   We respect honour, dignity and our mother tongue.
   We pass on our traditions, courage
   And our state to future generations.

   CHORUS

KENYA

Words written collectively

Composer unknown

Adopted on 12 December, 1963. Based on a traditional Kenya Folk Song which was adapted and harmonised by a National Commission of Five Musicians, who also wrote the words.

2. *Amkeni ndugu zetu*
   Tufanye sote bidii
   Nasi tujitoe kwa nguvu
   Nchiyetu ya Kenya tunayoipenda
   Tuwe tayari kuilinda.

3. *Natujenge taifa letu*
   Ee ndio wajibu wetu
   Kenya istahili heshima
   Tuungane mikono pamoja kazini
   Kila siku tuwe nashukrani.

2. Let one and all arise
   With hearts both strong and true.
   Service be our earnest endeavour,
   And our Homeland of Kenya,
   Heritage of splendour,
   Firm may we stand to defend.

3. Let all with one accord
   In common bond united,
   Build this our nation together,
   And the glory of Kenya,
   The fruit of our labour
   Fill every heart with thanksgiving.

KIRIBATI

Words and music by
URIUM TAMUERA IOTEBA (1910 - 1988)

First sung when independence was achieved on 12 July, 1979.

Ta - ua - ni - nne n te— ra - oi - roi, Ta - ngi - ri - a ao - ma - ta.

2. *Reken te kabaia ma te rau*
   Ibuakoia kaain abara
   Bon reken te nano ae banin
   Ma te i-tangitangiri naba.
   Ma ni wakina te kab'aia,
   Ma n neboa i eta abara.
   Ma ni wakina te kab'aia,
   Ma n neboa abara.

3. *Ti butiko ngkoe Atuara*
   Kawakinira ao kairira
   Nakon taai aika i maira.
   Buokira ni baim ae akoi.
   Kakabaia ara Tautaeka
   Ma ake a makuri iai.
   Kakabaia ara Tautaeka
   Ma aomata ni bane.

Translation

1. Stand up, Kiribati!
   Sing with jubilation!
   Prepare to accept responsibility
   And to help each other!
   Be steadfastly righteous!
   Love all our people!
   Be steadfastly righteous!
   Love all our people!

2. The attainment of contentment
   And peace by our people
   Will be achieved when all
   Our hearts beat as one,
   Love one another!
   Promote happiness and unity!
   Love one another!
   Promote happiness and unity!

3. We beseech You, O God,
   To protect and lead us
   In the days to come.
   Help us with Your loving hand.
   Bless our Government
   And all our people!
   Bless our Government
   And all our people!

KOREA (North)

Words by
PAK SE YONG (1902 - 1989)

Music by
KIM WON GYUN (1917 - 2002)

1. A ch'im ŭn pin na - ra i kang - san Ŭn -
gum e, cha - wŏn do ka - dŭk han Sam - ch'ol - li, a - rŭm - da - un
nae cho - guk, Pan - man - nyŏn ora - en ryŏk - sa e. Ch'al -

Adopted in 1947.

2. *Paektusan kisang ŭl ta anko.*
   Kŭllo ŭi chŏngsin ŭn kittŭrŏ.
   Chilli ro mungch 'yŏ jin ŏksen ttŭt
   On segye apsŏ nagari.
   Sonnŭn him nodo do naemirŏ,
   Inmin ŭi ttŭs ŭro sŏn nara.
   Han ŏpsi pugang hanŭn
   I chosŏn kiri pinnaese.

Translation

1. Let morning shine on the silver and gold of this land,
   Three thousand leagues packed with natural wealth.
   My beautiful fatherland.
   The glory of a wise people
   Brought up in a culture brilliant
   With a history five millennia long.
   Let us devote our bodies and minds
   To supporting this Korea for ever.

2. The firm will, bonded with truth,
   Nest for the spirit of labour,
   Embracing the atmosphere of Mount Paektu,
   Will go forth to all the world.
   The country established by the will of the people,
   Breasting the raging waves with soaring strength.
   Let us glorify for ever this Korea,
   Limitlessly rich and strong.

KOREA (South)
Aegukka

Words by
YUN CH'I-HO (1865 - 1946)
or AN CH'ANG-HO (1878 - 1938)

Music by
AHN EAKTAY (1905 - 1965)

Andante maestoso

1. Tong - hai mool - kwa paik - tu - san - i Ma - ru - go tal - to - rok

Ha - na - nim - i po - ho - ha - sa U - ri na - ra man - sei.

Officially adopted on 15 August, 1948.

CHORUS

molto cresc.

Moo - gung-wha sam - chul-ri Hwa-ryu kang - san,

molto cresc.

13

Tae - han sa-ram tae-han__ eu-ro Ki - ri po-chun-ha - sae.

17

2. *Namsan uye chusonamu*
   Chulkapeul turultut.
   Paramisul pulbyunhamum
   Uri kisang ilsae.

   CHORUS

English versification by Whami Koh and T. M. Cartledge

1. Tong-Hai Sea and Pakdoo Mountain, so long as they endure,
   May God bless Korea our land for endless ages to come!

   CHORUS
   North to south bedecked with flowers, land of beauty rare,
   May God keep our country united and preserve our land.

2. Eternally Naamsaan's pine-trees stand like an armour sure,
   Through whatever tempest or danger, as our symbol of strength.

   CHORUS

308

KUWAIT

Words by
AHMAD MUSHARI AL-ADWANI (1923 - 1992)

Music by
IBRAHIM NASIR AL-SOULA (*b*. 1935)
Arr. by W. L. REED

Adopted in 1978.

1. *Watanil Kuwait Salemta Lilmajdi*
   Wa Ala Jabeenoka Tali-Ossaadi
   Watanil Kuwait
   Watanil Kuwait
   Watanil Kuwait Salemta Lilmajdi.

2. *Ya Mahda Abaa-il Ola Katabou*
   Sefral Khloudi Fanadati Shohobo
   Allaho Akbar Ehnahom Arabo
   Talaat Kawakebo Jannatil Kholdi
   Watanil Kuwait Salemta Lilmajdi.

3. *Bourekta Ya Watanil Kuwaita Lana*
   Sakanan Wa Eshta Alal Mada Watana
   Yafdeeka Horron Fi Hemaka Bana
   Sarhol Hayati Be Akramil Aydi
   Watanil Kuwait Salemta Lilmajdi.

4. *Nahmeeka Ya Watani Wa Shahidona*
   Sharoul Hoda Wal Haqqo Ra-Edona
   Wa Amirona Lil Ezzi Qa-Edona
   Rabbol Hamiyati Sadqol Waadi
   Watanil Kuwait Salemta Lilmajdi.

Translation

1. Kuwait, Kuwait, Kuwait,
   My country,
   In peace live, in dignity,
   Your face bright,
   Your face bright,
   Your face bright with majesty,
   Kuwait, Kuwait, Kuwait,
   My country.

2. Oh cradle of ancestry,
   Who put down its memory
   With everlasting symmetry,
   Showing all eternity,
   Those Arabs were Heavenly,
   Kuwait, Kuwait, Kuwait,
   My country.

3. Blessed be
   My country,
   A homeland for harmony,
   Warded by true sentry,
   Giving their souls aptly,
   Building high its history,
   Kuwait, Kuwait, Kuwait,
   My country.

4. We're for you, My country,
   Led by faith and loyalty,
   With its Prince equally,
   Fencing us all fairly,
   With warm love and verity,
   Kuwait, Kuwait, Kuwait,
   My country,
   In peace live, in dignity.

KYRGYZSTAN

Words by
DJAMIL SADYKOV (*b.* 1932)
and ESHMAMBET KULUEV (*b.* 1942)

Music by
NASYR DAVLESOV (*b.* 1929)
and KALYI MOLDOBASANOV (*b.* 1929)
Arr. by W. L. REED

Adopted on 18 December, 1992.

1. Vysokie gory, doliny, polia,
   Rodnaia, zavetnaia nasha zemlia,
   Otsy nashi zhili sredi Ala-Too
   Vsegda svoiu rodinu sviato khrania.

   CHORUS
   Vpered, kyrgzskii narod,
   Putem svobody vpered
   Vzrastai, narod, rastsvetai,
   Svoiu sud'bu sozidai.

2. Izvechno narod nash dlia druzby otkryt
   Edinstvo i druzhbu on v serdtse khranit
   Zemlia Kyrgyzstana rodnaia strana
   Luchami soglasia ozarena.

   CHORUS

3. Mechty i nadezhdy naroda sbylis'
   I znamia svobody voznositsia vvys'.
   Nasled'e otsov nashikh peredadim
   Na blago naroda potomkam svoim.

   CHORUS

Translation

1. High mountains, valleys and fields
   Are our native, holy land.
   Our fathers lived amidst the Ala-Toe,
   Always saving their motherland.

   CHORUS
   Come on, Kyrgyz people,
   Come on to freedom!
   Stand up and flourish!
   Create your fortune!

2. We are open for freedom for ages.
   Friendship and unity are in our hearts.
   The land of Kyrgyzstan, our native state,
   Shining in the rays of consent.

   CHORUS

3. Dreams of the people came true,
   And the flag of liberty is over us.
   The heritage of our fathers we will
   Pass to our sons for the benefit of people.

   CHORUS

LAOS
Pheng Xat Lao
(Hymn of the Lao People)

Words by
SISANA SISANE (1922 - 1999)

Music by
THONGDY SOUNTHONEVICHIT (1905 - 1968)

Xat - lao tang-tae day - ma lao thook-thua - na xeut-xoo soo-

tchay, Huam - haeng huam-chit huam - chay sa-mak-khi - kan pen kam-lang di-

ao. Det - diao phom-kan kao - na boo - xa xü - kiat khong

Adopted in 1947. New text adopted in 1975.

Translation

For all time the Lao people have glorified their Fatherland,
United in heart, spirit and vigour as one.
Resolutely moving forwards,
Respecting and increasing the dignity of the Lao people
And proclaiming the right to be their own masters.
The Lao people of all origins are equal
And will no longer allow imperialists and traitors to harm them.
The entire people will safeguard the independence
And the freedom of the Lao nation.
They are resolved to struggle for victory
In order to lead the nation to prosperity.

LATVIA

Words and music by
KARLIS BAUMANIS (1834 - 1904)

Dievs, svē ti Lat vi ju, Mūs' dār go tē vi ju,

Svē ti jel Lat vi ju, Ak svē ti jel to!

to! Kur lat vju mei tas zied, Kur lat vju

Originally written as an entry for a singing festival in 1873, it very soon became the National Anthem.

dē li dzied, Laid mums tur lat mē diet, Mūs

Lat vi jā. Lat vi jā.

Versification by George A. Simons

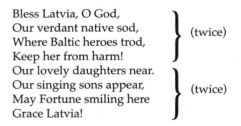

Bless Latvia, O God,
Our verdant native sod,
Where Baltic heroes trod,
Keep her from harm!
Our lovely daughters near.
Our singing sons appear,
May Fortune smiling here
Grace Latvia!

(twice)

(twice)

LEBANON

Words by
RACHID NAKHLÉ (1873 - 1939)

Music by
WADIH SABRA (1876 - 1952)

1. *Koul - lou - na*   *Lil - oua - tann Lil - 'ou - la   Lil   'a*

Adopted officially on 12 July, 1927.

2. *Chaykhouna Oualfata Indasaôutil Oua Tann*
   Ousdou ghâ Bin Mata Saouarat Nalfitann
   Charkouna Kalbouhou Aba Dann Loubnane
   Sanahou Rab Bouhou Limadal Azmane.
   Koullouna Lilouatann Lil' Oula Lil 'Alam,
   Koullouna Lilouatann.

3. *Bahrouhou Barrouhou Dourratouchchar Kain*
   Rildouhou Birrouhou Malioul Koutbaïn
   Ismouhou 'Izzouhou Moun Zou Kânal Joudoude
   Majdouhu Arzouhou Ramzouhou Lilkhouloude
   Koullouna Lilouatann Lil' Oula Lil 'Alam,
   Koullouna Lilouatann.

Translation

1. All of us! For our Country, for our Flag and Glory!
   Our valour and our writings are the envy of the ages.
   Our mountains and our valleys, they bring forth stalwart men.
   And to Perfection all our efforts we devote.
   All of us! For our Country, for our Flag and Glory!

2. Our Elders and our children, they await our Country's call:
   And on the Day of Crisis they are as Lions of the Jungle.
   The heart of our East is ever Lebanon:
   May God preserve her until end of time.
   All of us! For our Country, for our Flag and Glory!

3. The Gems of the East are her land and sea.
   Throughout the world her good deeds flow from pole to pole.
   And her name is her glory since time began.
   Immortality's Symbol - the Cedar - is her Pride.
   All of us! For our Country, for our Flag and Glory!

LESOTHO

Words by
FRANÇOIS COILLARD (1834 - 1904)

Music by
FERDINAND-SAMUEL LAUR (1791 - 1854)

1. Le - so - tho fa - tse la bo - nta - t'a ro - na, Ha - r'a ma - fa - tse le le - tle ke lo - na. Ke moo re hla - hi - leng, Ke moo re ho - li - leng, Re - a le ra - ta.

The Government adopted this as their National Anthem on 1 June, 1967, using the first and fifth verses of the words written by a French missionary.

324

2. *Molimo ak'u boloke Lesotho,*
   U felise lintoa le matšoenyeho.
   Oho fatše lena,
   La bo-ntat'a rona,
   Le be le khotso.

Translation

1. Lesotho, land of our Fathers,
   You are the most beautiful country of all.
   You give us birth,
   In you we are reared
   And you are dear to us.

2. Lord, we ask You to protect Lesotho.
   Keep us free from conflict and tribulations.
   Oh, land of mine,
   Land of our Fathers,
   May you have peace.

LIBERIA

Words by
DANIEL BASHIEL WARNER (1815 - 1880)

Music by
OLMSTEAD LUCA (1826 - 1869)

1. All hail, Li - be - ria, hail! All hail, Li - be - ria, hail! This glo - rious land of li - ber-ty Shall long be ours.—— Though new her name, Green be her fame, And migh - ty be her

Adopted on 26 July, 1847.

2. All hail, Liberia, hail!
   All hail, Liberia, hail!
   In union strong success is sure.
   We cannot fail!
   With God above
   Our rights to prove,
   We will o'er all prevail! } (twice)

   With heart and hand our country's cause defending,
   We'll meet the foe with valour unpretending.
   Long live Liberia, happy land!
   A home of glorious liberty }
   By God's command! } (twice)

LIBYA / LIBYAN ARAB JAMAHIRIYA

Words by
ABDALLA SHAMS EL-DIN (1921 - 1977)

Music by
MAHMOUD EL-SHERIF (1912 - 1990)
Arr. by W. L. REED

Al - la - hu Ak - bar____ Al - la - hu Ak - bar____ Al - la - hu

Adopted on 1 September, 1969.

Ak - bar Fau - qua Kai - di L'mu - ta - di_____ Al - la - hu

stacc.

Lil - maz - lu - mi Hai - rumu' ay - yi - di_____ Al - la - hu

1.

2.

___ A - na Bil - ya - qini Wa - bis - si - lahi Saaf - ta - di_____

___ Ba - ladi Wa - nu - ru L-haq - qi Yas - tau Fi Ya - di

Ya Hadihi Ddunya Atilli Wa 'Smai
Gaisu L-aadi Ga'a Yabgi Masrai
Bil-haqqi Saufa Fa-saufa Afnihi Mai.

Qulu Mai L-wailu Lil-mustamiri
Wa Llahu Fauqa L-gadiri L-mutagabbiri
Allahu Akbaru Ya Biladi Kabbiri
Wa-hudi Binasiyati L-mugiri Wa-dammiri.

Translation by M. A. S. Abdul Haleem

God is greatest!
God is greatest!
He is above the plots of the aggressors,
And He is the best helper of the oppressed.
With faith and with weapons I shall defend my country,
And the light of truth will shine in my hand.
Sing with me!
Sing with me!
God is greatest!
God is greatest!
God, God, God is greatest!
God is above the aggressors.

O World, look up and listen!
The enemy's army is coming,
Wishing to destroy me.
With truth and with my gun I shall repulse him.

And should I be killed,
I would kill him with me.
Sing with me –
Woe to the Imperialists!
And God is above the treacherous tyrant.
God is greatest!
Therefore glorify Him, O my country,
And seize the forehead of the tyrant
And destroy him!

LIECHTENSTEIN

Words by
JAKOB JOSEPH JAUCH (1802 - 1859)

Composer unknown *

The original five verses were written in 1850. The words were slightly changed in 1963, and only the first and last verses are currently used.
* The melody is the same as that of the National Anthem of the United Kingdom.

2. *Hoch lebe Liechtenstein,*
   Blühend am jungen Rhein,
   Glücklich und treu.
   Hoch leb'der Fürst vom Land,
   Hoch unser Vaterland,
   Durch Bruderliebe-Band ⎱ (twice)
   Vereint und frei. ⎰

Translation

1. High above the young Rhine
   Lies Liechtenstein, resting
   On Alpine heights.
   This beloved homeland,
   This dear fatherland
   Was chosen for us by ⎱ (twice)
   God's wise hand. ⎰

2. Long live Liechtenstein,
   Blossoming on the young Rhine,
   Happy and faithful!
   Long live the Prince of the Land,
   Long live our fatherland, ⎱ (twice)
   United by brotherly bonds and free! ⎰

LITHUANIA
Tautiska Giesme
(National Song)

Words and music by
VINCAS KUDIRKA (1858 - 1899)

First appeared in print in 1896.
Became the National Anthem in 1918.

Tam - su - mus pra - ša - li - na   Ir švie - sa   ir tie - sa
De - ga mū - sų šir - dy-se   Var - dan tos   Lie - tu - vos

1. Mūs žings-nius te - ly - di   2. Vie - ny-bė te - žy - di!

Versification

1. Lithuania, land of heroes,
   Thou our Fatherland that art,
   From the glorious deeds of ages
   Shall Thy children take heart.
   May Thy children ever follow
   Their heroic fathers
   In devotion to their country
   And good will to others.

2. May the sun of our loved shore
   Shine upon us evermore;
   May the right and the truth
   Keep our pathway lighted.
   May the love of our dear land
   Make us strong of heart and hand,
   May our land ever stand
   Peaceful and united.

LUXEMBOURG
Ons Heemecht
(Our Homeland)

Words by
MICHEL LENTZ (1820 - 1893)

Music by
JEAN-ANTOINE ZINNEN (1827 - 1898)
Arr. by MARTIN SHAW

1. Wou d'Uel - zecht du - rech d'Wi - sen zéit, Duerch d'Fiel - sen d'Sau - er brëcht. Wou d'Rief laanscht d'Mu - sel dof - teg bléit, Den Him - mel Wäin ons mëcht. Dat

First performed on 5 June, 1864, this became the National Anthem in 1895. There are four verses in all.
Luxembourg also has a Royal Anthem (music adopted in 1883 and the words adopted in 1919) with words by
Nikolaus Welter (1871 - 1951) the music is by an unknown composer.

2. *O Du do uewen, deem séng Hand*
   Duurch d'Welt d'Natioune leet,
   Behitt Du d'Lëtzebuerger Land
   Vru friemem Joch a Leed!
   Du hues ons all als Kanner schon
   De fräie Geescht jo gin.
   Looss viru blénken d'Fräiheetssonn,
   Déi mir sou laang gesin.

Translation by Fabio Lazzati

1. Where the Alzette flows through the meadows,
   The Sura breaks through the crags.
   Where the vine fragrant grows along the Moselle,
   The sky promises us wine:
   There lies the land for which we willingly
   Dare everything down here.
   Our Homeland which we so deeply
   Carry in our hearts.

2. O Thou above, Whose powerful hand
   Leads athe nations through the world,
   Protect the Luxembourg land
   From foreign yoke and threat.
   As children Thou already instilled in us all
   The spirit of freedom.
   Let freedom's sun, which we have known for so long,
   Shine for evermore.

French version

1. *Où l'Alzette arrose champs et prés,*
   La Sûre baigne les rochers;
   Où la Moselle, riante et belle,
   Nous fait cadeau du vin,
   C'est notre pays pour lequel
   Nous risquons tout sur terre;
   Notr' chère et adorable partie
   Dont notr' âme est remplie.

2. *O Toi aux cieux qui nuit et jour*
   Diriges les nations du monde;
   Écarte du pays de Luxembourg
   L'oppression étrangère
   Enfants nous avons reçu de Toi
   L'esprit de la liberté.
   Permets au soleil de liberté
   De luire à tout jamais.

Translation by Fabio Lazzati

1. Where the Alzette waters fields and meadows,
   The Sura washes the crags;
   Where the Moselle, smiling and beautiful,
   Presents us with wine:
   That is our land for which
   We dare everything down here;
   Our dear and adorable Motherland,
   With which our heart is filled.

2. O Thou in heaven, Who night and day
   Leadest the nations of the world;
   Avert from the land of Luxembourg
   The foreign yoke.
   As children we received from You
   The spirit of freedom.
   Let freedom's sun
   Shine for evermore.

MACEDONIA

Words by
VLADO MALESKI (1919 - 1984)

Music by
TODOR SKALOVSKI (1909 - 2004)

1. De - nes nad Ma - ke - do - ni - ja se ra - gja

No - vo son - ce — na slo - bo - da - ta, — Ma - ke -

don - ci - te se bo - rat — Za — svoj - te prav - di -

Officially adopted on 11 August, 1992.

ni,_____ Ma - ke - don - ci - te se bo - rat_____ Za_____

19

svoj - te prav - di - ni._____ 2. Od - zi - ve - e._____

1. and 2.

3.

25

2. *Odnovo sega znameto se vee*
   Na Krusevskata Republika
   Goce Delcev, Pitu Guli,
   Dame Gruev, Sandanski. } *(twice)*

3. *Gorite Makedonski sumno peat*
   Novi pesni, novi vesnici,
   Makedonija slobodna
   Slobodna zivee. } *(twice)*

Translation by T. Dragadze

1. Today over Macedonia
   A new sun of freedom rises,
   Macedonians fight
   For their rights. } (twice)

2. Now once again flies
   The flag of the Krusevo Republic,
   Goce Delcev, Pitu Guli,
   Dame Gruev, Sandanski. } (twice)

3. The Macedonian woodlands sing brightly
   New songs, new awakenings.
   Free Macedonia
   Lives free. } (twice)

MADAGASCAR

Words by
Pasteur RAHAJASON (1897 - 1971)

Music by
NORBERT RAHARISOA (1873 - 1964)
Arr. by HENRY COLEMAN

Adopted on 21 October, 1958.

2. *Ry Tanindrazanay malala ô*
   Irinay mba hanompoan'anao.
   Ny tena sy fo fanahy anananay 'zay sarobidy
   Sy mendrika tokoa.

   CHORUS

3. *Ry Tanindrazanay malala ô*
   Irinay mba hitahian' anao.
   Ka Ilay Nahary 'zao ton tolo izao no
   Fototra ijoroan, ny satanao.

   CHORUS

Translation

1. O, our beloved fatherland,
   O, fair Madagascar,
   Our love will never decay,
   But will last eternally.

   CHORUS
   O, Lord Creator, do Thou bless
   This Island of our Fathers,   ⎫
   That she may be happy and prosperous ⎬ (twice)
   For our own satisfaction.   ⎭

2. O, our beloved fatherland,
   Let us be thy servant
   With body, heart and spirit
   In dear and worthy service.

   CHORUS

3. O, our beloved fatherland,
   May God bless thee,
   That created all lands;
   In order He maintains thee.

   CHORUS

MALAWI

Words* and music by
MICHAEL-FREDRICK PAUL SAUKA (*b.* 1934)

With devotion

1. *Mlu - ngu da - li - tsa - ni Ma - la - wi,*
1. O God bless our land of Ma - la - wi,

Mum - su - nge m'mte - nde - re. Go - nje - tsa - ni
Keep it a land of peace. Put down each and

a - da - ni o - nse, Nja - la, nthe - nda, nsa - nje.
ev - 'ry e - ne - my, Hung - er, dis - ease, en - vy.

* The official text is given in Chichewa and English. The Chitumbuka version is no longer used.
Selected as a result of a competition held in February 1964, and first played publicly on Independence Day, 6 July, 1964.

2. *Malawi ndziko lokongola,*
   La chonde ndi ufulu,
   Nyanja ndi mphepo ya m'mapiri,
   Ndithudi tadala.
   Zigwa, mapiri, nthaka, dzinthu,
   N'mphatso zaulere.
   Nkhalango, madambo abwino.
   Ngwokoma Malawi.

3. *O Ufulu tigwirizane,*
   Kukweza Malawi.
   Ndi chikondi, khama, kumvera,
   Timutumikire.
   Pa nkhondo nkana pa mtendere,
   Cholinga n'chimodzi.
   Mai, bambo, tidzipereke,
   Pokweza Malawi.

Versification

2. Our own Malawi, this land so fair,
   Fertile and brave and free.
   With its lakes, refreshing mountain air,
   How greatly blest are we.
   Hills and valleys, soil so rich and rare
   Give us a bounty free.
   Wood and forest, plains so broad and fair,
   All - beauteous Malawi.

3. Freedom ever, let us all unite
   To build up Malawi.
   With our love, our zeal and loyalty,
   Bringing our best to her.
   In time of war, or in time of peace,
   One purpose and one goal.
   Men and women serving selflessly
   In building Malawi.

MALAYSIA

Words by
TUNKU ABDUL RAHMAN (1903 - 1990)

Music by
PIERRE JEAN DE BERANGER (1780 - 1857) *

Adopted when Malaya achieved independence on 31 August, 1957.

*It was previously known in Malaya and Indonesia as a popular song called 'Terang Bulan' (Moonlight), but this popular version of the tune is now banned. When Malaysia was founded in 1963 this was retained as the National Anthem. Malaysia also has thirteen State Anthems.

Translation

My country, my native land.
The people living united and progressive,
May God bestow blessing and happiness.
May our Ruler have a successful reign.
May God bestow blessing and happiness.
May our Ruler have a successful reign.

THE MALDIVES

Words by
MOHAMED JAMEEL DIDI (1915 - 1989)

Music by
PANDIT WANNAKUWATTAWADUGE
DON AMARADEVA (*b.* 1927)
Arr. by W. L. REED

The music was composed and adopted in 1972. There are eight verses.

Translation

CHORUS
In National Unity do we salute our Nation.
In the National language do we offer our prayers
And salute our Nation.

1. We bow in respect to the Emblem of our Nation,
   And salute the Flag so exalted.

CHORUS

2. We salute the colours of our Flag;
   Green, Red and White,
   Which symbolise Victory, Blessing and Success.

CHORUS

MALI

Words by
SEYDOU BADIAN KOUYATÉ (*b.* 1928)

Music by
BANZOUMANA SISSOKO (1890 - 1987)
Arr. by HENRY COLEMAN

Adopted on 9 August, 1962.

mi dé-couvre son front   Au de-dans ou au de-hors   Debout sur les rem-parts   Nous som-mes ré-so-lus de mou-rir.

CHORUS

_f_

Pour l'A -- frique et pour toi, Ma - li,
li d'au - jour -d'hui,   O   Ma - li,   de   de - main   Les champs fleu-

_f_

rall. 2nd time

1.

No - tre dra-peau___ se - ra li - ber - té.
ris - sent d'es- pé - ran - ce,   Les   coeurs vi- brent de con-

rall. 2nd time

353

Pour l'A - frique et pour toi Ma - li No - tre com - bat

se - ra u - ni - té. O Ma - fian - ce.

2. *Debout, villes et campagnes,*
   Debout, femmes, jeunes et vieux
   Pour la Patrie en marche
   Vers l'avenir radieux
   Pour notre dignité.
   Renforçons bien nos rangs,
   Pour le salut public
   Forgeons le bien commun
   Ensemble, au coude à coude
   Faisons le chantier du bonheur.

   CHORUS

3. *La voie est dure, très dure*
   Qui mène au bonheur commun.
   Courage et dévouement
   Vigilance à tout moment,
   Courage et dévouement
   Vigilance à tout moment,
   Vérité des temps anciens,
   Vérité de tous les jours,
   Le bonheur par le labeur
   Fera la Mali de demain.

   CHORUS

4. *L'Afrique se lève enfin*
   Saluons ce jour nouveau.
   Saluons la liberté,
   Marchons vers l'unité.
   Dignité retrouvée
   Soutient notre combat.
   Fidelès à notre serment
   De faire l'Afrique unie
   Ensemble, debout mes frères
   Tous au rendez-vous de l'honneur.

   CHORUS

Translation by T. M. Cartledge

1. At your call, Mali,
   So that you may prosper,
   Faithful to your destiny,
   We shall all be united,
   One people, one goal, one faith
   For a united Africa.
   If the enemy should show himself
   Within or without,
   On the ramparts,
   We are ready to stand and die.

   CHORUS
   For Africa and for you, Mali,
   Our banner shall be liberty.
   For Africa and for you, Mali,
   Our fight shall be for unity.
   Oh, Mali of today,
   Oh, Mali of tomorrow,
   The fields are flowering with hope
   And hearts are thrilling with confidence.

2. Stand up, towns and countryside,
   Stand up, women, stand up young and old,
   For the Fatherland on the road
   Towards a radiant future.
   For the sake of our dignity
   Let us strengthen our ranks;
   For the public well-being
   Let us forge the common good.
   Together, shoulder to shoulder,
   Let us work for happiness.

   CHORUS

3. The road is hard, very hard,
   That leads to common happiness.
   Courage and devotion,
   Constant vigilance,
   Courage and devotion,
   Constant vigilance,
   Truth from olden times,
   The truths of every day,
   Happiness through effort
   Will build the Mali of tomorrow.

   CHORUS

4. Africa is at last arising,
   Let us greet this new day.
   Let us greet freedom,
   Let us march towards unity.
   Refound dignity
   Supports our struggle.
   Faithful to our oath
   To make a united Africa,
   Together, arise, my brothers,
   All to the place where honour calls.

   CHORUS

MALTA
Innu Malti
(Hymn of Malta)

Words by
DUN KARM PSAILA (1871 - 1961)

Music by
ROBERT SAMMUT (1870 - 1934)

1. Lil din l-Art ħelwa, l'omm li tatna isimha, Ħares, Mulej, kif dejjem Int ħarist:

Dun Karm Psaila was asked to write these words for a school hymn to Sammut's music. He conceived the idea of writing a hymn to Malta in the form of a prayer; he wanted to unite all parties with the strong ties of religion and love of country.

It was first performed on 3 February, 1923, and officially became the National Anthem in 1945.

Fta - kar li lil - ha bl - oħ - la dawl— lib— bist!

2. *Agħti, kbir Alla, iddeħen lil min jaħkimha,*
   Rodd ilħniena lissid ,saħħa 'lħaddiem:
   Seddaq ilgħaqda fil-Maltin u ssliem!

Translation by May Butcher

1. Guard her, O Lord, as ever Thou has guarded,
   This Motherland so dear whose name we bear!
   Keep her in mind whom Thou has made so fair!

2. May he who rules for wisdom be regarded,
   In master mercy, strength in man increase!
   Confirm us all in unity and peace!

MARSHALL ISLANDS
Forever Marshall Islands

Words and music by
AMATA KABUA (1928 - 1995)
Arr. by W. L. REED

Ae - loñ eo āō ion lo - me - to;
My is - land lies o'er the ___ o - cean;

Ein - wot wut ko lōti ion dren ___ e - lae; Kin me - ram in
Like a wreath of flowers up - on ___ the sea; With the light of

Me - kar jen ijo ___ i - lañ; Err - eo an romak ioir kin me - ram -
Me - kar from far ___ a - bove; Shin - ing with the bril - liance of rays ___

MAURITANIA

Words by
BABA OULD CHEIKH (*d.* 1934) *

Music by
TOLIA NIKIPROWETZKY (1916 - 1997)

Based on traditional music, and adopted in 1960.

* Date of birth unknown.

D.%. al Fine

363

Kun lil-ilahi nasiran,   wa-ankir al-manakira
Wa-kun maaa l-haqqi l-ladhi   yarda-hu minka da'ira
Wa-la ta uuddu nafiaa   siwa-hu aw da'ira
Wa-sluk sabila l-mustafa   wa-mutt aalayhi sa'ira
Fa-ma kafa awwalana   a-laysa yakfi l-akhira
Wa-kun li-qawmin ahdathu   fi amrihi muhajira
Qad mawwahu bi-shibbin   waa-tadhiru ma aadhira,
Wa-za aamu maza iima   wa-sawwadu dafatira,
Wa-htanaku ahla l-fala,   wa-htanaku l-hawadira
Wa-awrathat akabira   bid aatuha asaghira
Wa-in da aa mujadilun   fi-amri-him ila mira
Fa-la tumari fihim   illa mira'a zahira

Translation by Joachim Kolb

Be a helper for God and censure what is forbidden,
And turn with the law which He wants you to follow,
Hold no one to be useful or harmful, except for Him,
And walk the path of the chosen one, and die while you are on it!
For what was sufficient for the first of us, is sufficient for the last one, too,
And leave those people who do evil things with respect to God.
They misrepresented him by making him similar, and made all kinds of excuses.
They made bold claims, and blackened notebooks.
They let the nomads and the sedentary people both make bitter experiences,
And the great sins of their [doctrinal] innovations bequeathed small.
And just in case a disputant calls you to dispute about their claims,
Do not, then, dispute on them, except by way of an external dispute.

MAURITIUS
Motherland

Words by
JEAN GEORGES PROSPER (*b.* 1933)

Music by
PHILIPPE GENTIL (*b.* 1928)

Selected by means of a competition, and came into use when the country attained independence on 12 March, 1968.

MEXICO

Words by
FRANCISCO GONZÁLEZ BOCANEGRA (1824 - 1861)

Music by
JAIME NUNÓ (1824 - 1908)

Lyrics:
Me - xi - ca - nos al gri - to_ de gue - rra El a-
ce - ro a - pre-stad y el bri - dón,_____ Y re-
tiem - ble en sus cen - tros la tie - rra, Al so-

Adopted on 16 September, 1854. There are four verses.

no - ro ru-gir del— ca-ñón,   Y re-

tiem - ble en sus cen - tros la tie - rra,   Al so-

FINE

no - ro ru-gir del— ca - ñón.

FINE

p **VERSE**

1. Ci - ña ¡oh Pa - tria! tus sie - nes de o - li - va   De la

p

paz___ el ar - cán - gel di - vi - no, Que en el

cie - lo tu e - ter - no des - ti - no Por el

de - do de Dios se es - cri - bió. Mas si o-

sa - re un ex - tra - ño e - ne - mi - go Pro - fa-

nar___ con su plan - ta tu sue - lo, Pien - sa ¡oh

Pa - tria que - ri - da! que el cie - lo Un sol-

da - do en ca - da hi - jo te dió, Un___ sol -

D.C. al Fine

da - do en ca - da hi - jo te dió.

D.C. al Fine

ff

370

2. *¡Patria! ¡Patria! Tus hijos te juran*
   Exhalar en tus aras su aliento,
   Si el clarín, con su bélico acento,
   Los convoca a lidiar con valor.
   ¡Para ti las guirnaldas de oliva!
   ¡Un recuerdo para ellos de gloria!
   ¡Un laurel para ti de victoria!
   ¡Un sepulcro para ellos de honor! } *(twice)*

CHORUS

Translation by T. M. Cartledge

CHORUS
Mexicans, when the war cry is heard,
Have sword and bridle ready.
Let the earth's foundations tremble } (twice)
At the loud cannon's roar.

1. May the divine archangel crown your brow,
   Oh fatherland, with an olive branch of peace,
   For your eternal destiny has been written
   In heaven by the finger of God.
   But should a foreign enemy
   Dare to profane your soil with his tread,
   Know, beloved fatherland, that heaven gave you
   A soldier in each of your sons.   } (twice)

CHORUS

2. Fatherland, oh fatherland, your sons vow
   To give their last breath on your altars,
   If the trumpet with its warlike sound
   Calls them to valiant battle.
   For you, the garlands of olive,
   For them, a glorious memory.
   For you, the victory laurels,
   For them, an honoured tomb.   } (twice)

CHORUS

MICRONESIA

Author unknown

Composer unknown

1. 'Tis here we are pledg - ing, with heart and with hand,
Full mea - sure of de - vo - tion to thee, our native land,
Full mea - sure of de - vo - tion to thee, our native land.

2. Now all join the chorus, let union abide.
Across all Micronesia join hands on every side.   } (twice)

3. We all work together, with hearts, voice and hand,
Till we have made these islands another promised land.   } (twice)

Adopted 10 December, 1991.

MOLDOVA
Limba Noastră
(Our Tongue)

Words by
ALEXEI MATEEVICI (*b.* 1962)

Music by
ALEXANDRU CRISTI (*b.* 1955)
Arr. by W. L. REED

Officially adopted on 7 June, 1994.

1. Limba noastră-i o comoară
   Iñ adîncuri înfundată,
   Un sirag de piatră rapă
   Pe mosie revărsată.
   Limba noastră-i foc ce arde
   Intr-un neam, ce fără veste
   S-a trezit din somn de moarte
   Ca viteazul din poveste.
   Limba noastră-i numai cîntec,
   Doina dorurilor noastre,
   Roi de fulgere, ce spintec
   Nouri negri, zări albastre.

2. Limba noastră-i graiul pîinii,
   Cînd de vînt se mişcă vara;
   Iñ rostirea ei bătrînii
   Cu sudori sfinţit-au ţara.
   Limba noastră-i frunză verde,
   Zbuciumul din codrii veşnici,
   Nistrul lin, ce-n valuri pierde
   Ai luceferilor sfeşnici.
   Nu veţi plînge-atunci amarnic,
   Că vi-i limba prea săracă,
   Si-ţi vedea, cît îi de darnic
   Graiul ţării noastre dragă.

3. Limba noastră-i vechi izvoade.
   Povestiri din alte vremuri;
   Şi citindu-le 'nşirate, –
   Te-nfiori adînc şi tremuri.
   Limba noastră îi aleasă
   Să ridice slavă-n ceruri,
   Să ne spiue-n hram şi-acasă
   Veşnicele adevăruri.
   Limba noastră-i limba sfîntă,
   Limba vechilor cazanii,
   Care o plîng şi care o cîntă
   Pe la vatra lor ţăranii.

4. Iñviaţi-vă dar graiul,
   Ruginit de multă vreme,
   Ştergeţi slinul, mucegaiul
   Al uitării 'n care geme.
   Strîngeţi piatra lucitoare
   Ce din soare se aprinde –
   Şi-ţi avea în revărsare
   Un potop nou de cuvinte.
   Răsări-va o comoară
   Iñ adîncuri înfundată,
   Un şirag de piatră rară
   Pe moşie revărsată.

374

Translation

1. A treasure is our tongue that surges
   From deep shadows of the past,
   Chain of precious stones that scattered
   All over our ancient land.
   A burning flame is our tongue
   Amidst a people waking
   From a deathly sleep, no warning,
   Like the brave man of the stories.
   Our tongue is made of songs
   From our soul's deepest desires,
   Flash of lightning striking swiftly
   Through dark clouds and blue horizons.

2. Our tongue is the tongue of bread
   When the winds blow through the summer,
   Uttered by our forefathers who
   Blessed the country through their labour.
   Our tongue is the greenest leaf
   Of the everlasting forests,
   Gentle river Nistru's ripples
   Hiding starlight bright and shining.
   Utter no more bitter cries now
   That your language is too poor,
   And you will see with what abundance
   Flow the words of our precious country.

3. Our tongue is full of legends,
   Stories from the days of old.
   Reading one and then another
   Makes one shudder, tremble and moan.
   Our tongue is singled out
   To lift praises up to heaven,
   Uttering with constant fervour
   Truths that never cease to beckon.
   Our tongue is more than holy,
   Words of homilies of old
   Wept and sung perpetually
   In the homesteads of our folks.

4. Resurrect now this our language,
   Rusted through the years that have passed,
   Wipe off filth and mould that gathered
   When forgotten through our land.
   Gather now the sparkling stone,
   Catching bright light from the sun.
   You will see the endless flooding
   Of new words that overflow.
   A treasure will spring up swiftly
   From deep shadows of the past,
   Chain of precious stones that scattered
   All over our ancient land.

MONACO

Words by
LOUIS NOTARI (1879 - 1961)

Music by
CHARLES ALBRECHT (1817 - 1895)

First performed in 1867 when it was officially adopted along with the original words by the composer. New Monégasque words were adopted in 1931.

Despoei tugiù, sciü d'u nostru paise
Se ride aù ventu, u meme pavayun
Despoei tugiù a curù russa e gianca
E stàr r'emblèma d'a nostra libertà
Grandi e piciui, r'an tugiù respeta.

French Translation

Depuis toujours, sur notre pays,
Le même drapeau est déployé au vent,
Depuis toujours les couleurs rouge et blanche
Sont le symbole de notre liberté
Grands et petits les ont toujours respectées.

English Translation

All the time, over our country,
The same flag has been flying in the wind
All the time, the colours red and white
Have been the symbol of our liberty
Great and small have always respected them.

MONGOLIA

Words by
TSENDIIN DAMDINSUREN (1908 - 1986)

Music by
BILEGIIN DAMDINSUREN (1919 - 1991)
and LUVSANJAMTS MURJORJ (1919 - 1996)

The words and music were adopted in 1950, replacement words were adopted in 1961 and the original words were restored in 1991. The National Anthem is expected to be replaced in the near future.

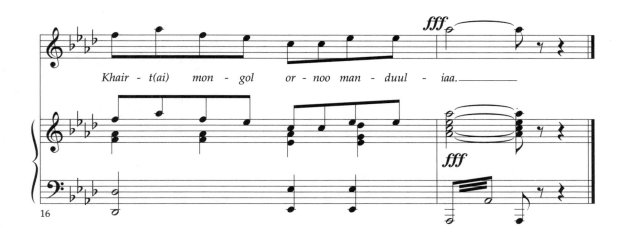

Khair - t(ai) mon - gol or - noo man - duul - iaa._____

2. *Zorigt mongolyn zoltoi arduud*
   Zovlong tonilgozh zhargalyg edlev
   Zhargalyn tulkhuur khogzhliin tulguur
   Zhavkhlant manai oron mandtugai.

   CHORUS

Translation by D. Altangorel

1. Our sacred revolutionary country
   Is the ancestral hearth of all Mongols,
   No enemy will defeat us,
   And we will prosper for eternity.

   CHORUS
   Our country will strengthen relations
   With all righteous countries of the world.
   And let us develop our beloved Mongolia
   With all our will and might.

2. The glorious people of the brave Mongolia
   Have defeated all sufferings, and gained happiness,
   The key to delight, and the path to progress –
   Majestic Mongolia – our country, live forever!

   CHORUS

MOROCCO

Words by
ALI SQUALLI HOUSSAINI (*b.* 1932)

Music by
LÉO MORGAN (1919 - 1984)
Arr. by W. L. REED

The music was adopted in 1956, the words in 1970.
The National Anthem of Morocco is also used in Western Sahara.

Translation

Fountain of Freedom	Source of Light
Where sovereignty and safety meet,	
Safety and sovereignty	May you ever combine!
You have lived among nations	With title sublime,
Filling each heart,	Sung by each tongue,
Your champion has risen	And answered your call.
In my mouth	And in my blood
Your breezes have stirred	Both light and fire.
Up! my brethren,	Strive for the highest.
We call to the world	That we are here ready.
We salute as our emblem	
God, Homeland and King.	

MOZAMBIQUE

Pátria Amada
(Beloved Fatherland)

Words and music by
JUSTINO SIGAULANE CHEMANE (1923 - 2003)
Arr. by MARTIN WEHN

Na me-mó-ri-a de Á-fri-ca e do Mun-do, Pá-tria be-la dos qu' ou sa-ram lu-tar Mo-çam-bi-que o teu no-meé li-ber-da-de, O sol de Ju-nho pa-ra sem-pre bri-lha-rá! Mo-çam-

Adopted in 2002.

385

2. *Povo unido do Rovuma ao Maputo,*
   Colhe os frutos do combate pela Paz!
   Cresce o sonho ondulando na Bandeira
   E val lavrando na certeza do amanhá!

   CHORUS

3. *Flores brotando do chão do teu suor,*
   Pelos montes, pelos rios, pelo mar!
   Nós juramos por ti, ó Moçambique:
   Nenhum tirano nos irá escravizar!

   CHORUS

Translation

1. Remembering Africa and the world
   You are the beautiful homeland of those who fought!
   Mozambique: your name is freedom
   May the sun of June shine forever!

   CHORUS
   Our Glorious homeland Mozambique
   Is building all the stones of tomorrow
   Millions of arms are one power
   O beloved homeland, we shall overcome!

2. United people from Rumova to Maputo
   You'll harvest the fruits of your peaceful battle!
   You may work in a safe morning
   While a dream is growing and the flag is waving!

   CHORUS

3. Flowers are blooming on the ground of your blood
   As on hills, rivers and on the sea!
   We vow to thee, O Mozambique:
   No tyrant will enslave us ever!

   CHORUS

MYANMAR

Words and music by
SAYA TIN (1914 - 1947)
Arr. by W. L. REED

Adopted officially in 1948.

Translation by T. M. Cartledge

We shall always love Burma,
Land of our forefathers. } (twice)
We fight and give our lives
For our union.
For her we responsibly shoulder the task,
Standing as one in duty to our precious land.

* The notes between asterisks may be sung an octave higher.
✹ At the end of the National Anthem it is customary for the singers to give a slight bow.

NAMIBIA

Words and music by
AXALI DOESEB (*b.* 1954)
Arr. by W. L. REED

Na-mi-bi-a, land of the brave, Free-dom's fight we have won. Glo-ry to their bra-ve-ry, Whose blood wa-ters our free-dom. We give our love and loy-al-ty

Adopted on 21 March, 1991, first anniversary of independence.

NAURU

Words by
MARGARET HENDRIE (1924 - 1990)

Music by
LAURENCE HENRY HICKS (1912- 1997)
Arr. by W. L. REED

Officially adopted in 1968.

yin ou - ge, Nau - ru e - ko do - gin!

Translation

Nauru our homeland, the land we dearly love,
We all pray for you and we also praise your name.
Since long ago you have been the home of our great forefathers
And will be for generations yet to come.
We all join in together to honour your flag,
And we shall rejoice together and say;
Nauru for evermore!

NEPAL

Words by
CHAKRAPANI CHALISE (1884 - 1959)

Music by
BAKHATBIR BUDHAPIRTHI (1857 - 1920)

Music adopted in 1899. Words adopted in 1924.

le   pra-jâ   phai - li - yos   pu-kâ-raun   ja-ya   pre-ma-le   Hâ -

mi   ne - pâ - li   bhâ - ee___ sâ - râ - le.

Translation

May glory crown you, courageous Sovereign,
You, the gallant Nepalese,
Shri Pansh Maharajadhiraja, our glorious ruler,
May he live for many years to come
And may the number of his subjects increase.
Let every Nepalese sing this with joy.

NETHERLANDS

Words by
PHILIP VAN MARNIX VON SINT ALGEGONDE (1540 - 1598)

Music by
ADRIAAN VALERIUS (1575 - 1625) *
Arr. by M. J. BRISTOW

Officially adopted on 10 May, 1932. There are fifteen verses in all, but only the first and sixth verses are sung.

* Melody known from before 1572. Song appeared in Valerius 'Nederlandtsche Gedenck - Clanck', 1626.

vrij on - ver - veert; Den Co - ninck van His -
pan - jen Heb ick al - tijd ghe - eert.

2. *Mijn schilt ende betrouwen*
   Zijt ghy, O Godt, mijn Heer,
   Op U soo wil ick bouwen,
   Verlaet my nimmermeer;
   Dat ick doch vroom mag blijven
   U dienaer t'aller stond,
   Die tyranny verdrijven,
   Die my mijn hert doorwondt.

Translation by T. M. Cartledge

1. William of Nassau am I, of Germanic descent;
   True to the fatherland I remain until death.
   Prince of Orange am I, free and fearless.
   To the King of Spain I have always given honour.

2. You, my God and Lord, are my shield, on You I rely.
   On You I will build; never leave me,
   So that I may remain pious, Your servant at all moments,
   Dispelling the tyranny that wounds my heart.

NEW ZEALAND
God Defend New Zealand

English words by
THOMAS BRACKEN (1843 - 1898)
Maori words by
THOMAS HENRY SMITH (1824 - 1907)

Music by
JOHN JOSEPH WOODS (1849 - 1934)

Officially adopted in Centennial Year, 1940. This National Anthem and the National Anthem of the United Kingdom were given equal status in 1977, as New Zealand's National Anthems. The National Anthem of New Zealand is also used in Niue and Tokelau. The Cook Islands have their own National Anthem.

Make her prais - es heard a - far, God de - fend New Zea - land.
Ma - na - a - ki - ti - a mai   A - o - te - a - ro - a.

2. Men of every creed and race
   Gather here before Thy face,
   Asking Thee to bless this place,
   God defend our free land.
   From dissension, envy, hate
   And corruption guard our State,
   Make our country good and great,
   God defend New Zealand.

3. Peace, not war, shall be our boast,
   But, should foes assail our coast,
   Make us then a mighty host,
   God defend our free land.
   Lord of battles, in Thy might,
   Put our enemies to flight,
   Let our cause be just and right,
   God defend New Zealand.

4. Let our love for Thee increase,
   May Thy blessings never cease,
   Give us plenty, give us peace,
   God defend our free land.
   From dishonour and from shame
   Guard our country's spotless name,
   Crown her with immortal fame,
   God defend New Zealand.

5. May our mountains ever be
   Freedom's ramparts on the sea,
   Make us faithful unto Thee,
   God defend our free land.
   Guide her in the nations' van,
   Preaching love and truth to man,
   Working out Thy glorious plan,
   God defend New Zealand.

2. *Ona mano tangata*
   Kiri whero, kiri ma,
   Iwi Maori Pakeha,
   Repeke katoa,
   Nei ka tono ko nga he
   Mau e whakaahu ke,
   Kia ora marire
   Aotearoa.

3. *Tona mana kia tu!*
   Tona kaha kia u;
   Tona rongo hei paku
   Ki te ao katoa,
   Aua rawa nga whawhai,
   Nga tutu a tata mai,
   Kia tupu nui ai
   Aotearoa.

4. *Waiho tona takiwa*
   Ko te ao marama;
   Kia whiti tona ra
   Taiawhio noa.
   Ko te hae me te ngangau
   Meinga kia kore kau;
   Waiho i te rongo mau
   Aotearoa.

5. *Tona pai toitu;*
   Tika rawa, pono pu;
   Tona noho, tana tu;
   Iwi no Ihoa.
   Kaua mona whakama;
   Kia hau te ingoa;
   Kia tu hei tauira;
   Aotearoa.

NICARAGUA

Words by
SALOMÓN IBARRA MAYORGA (1890 - 1985)

Music by
LUIS ABRAHAM DELGADILLO (1887 - 1961)

Adopted in 1918.
The words formerly sung were replaced by these words in 1939 by a government decree.

ma - nos Tu glo - rio - so pen - dón—— bi - co-

lor,—— Ni se ti - ñe con san - gre de her - ma-nos Tu glo-

rio - so pen - dón—— bi - co - lor. Bri - lle her-

mo - sa la paz—— en tu cie - lo, Na - da em-pa - ñe tu

Translation by T. M. Cartledge

Hail to you, Nicaragua.
The cannon's voice no longer roars,
Nor does the blood of our brothers
Stain your glorious bicoloured flag. } (twice)
Peace shines in beauty in your skies,
Nothing dims your immortal glory,
For work is what earns your laurels
And honour is your triumphal ensign.

403

NIGER
La Nigérienne
(The Song of Niger)

Words by
MAURICE ALBERT THIRIET (1906 - 1969)

Music by
ROBERT JACQUET (1896 - 1976) and
NICOLAS ABEL FRANÇOIS FRIONNET (1911 - 1998)

1. Au - près du grand Ni - ger puis - sant Qui rend la na - tu - re plus bel - le,

So - yons fiers et re - con - nais - sants De no - tre li - ber - té nou - vel - le.

Approved by the National Assembly in July, 1961, the year after independence.

Evitons les vaines querelles
Afin d'épargner notre sang;
Et que les glorieux accents
De notre race sans tutelle
S'élèvent dans un même élan
Jusqu'à ce ciel éblouissant
Où veille son âme éternelle
Qui fera le pays plus grand. De-

bout Ni-ger: De-bout!_____ Sur le sol et sur l'on - de, Au

ryth-me des tam-tams, dans leur son gran-dis-sant, Res-

tons u-nis, tou-jours,_____ et que cha-cun ré-pon - de A ce noble a-ve-

poco rall.

nir qui nous dit: "En_____ a-vant."_____

poco rall.

2. *Nous retrouvons dans nos enfants*
    Toutes les vertus des Ancêtres:
    Pour lutter dans tous les instants
    Elles sont notre raison d'être.
    Nous affrontons le fauve traître
    A peine armés le plus souvent,
    Voulant subsister dignement
    Sans detruire pour nous repaître.
    Dans la steppe où chacun ressent
    La soif, dans le Sahel brûlant,
    Marchons, sans défaillance, en maîtres
    Magnanimes et vigilants.

CHORUS

Translation by T. M. Cartledge

1. By the waters of the mighty Niger,
    Which adds to the beauty of nature,
    Let us be proud and grateful
    For our new-won liberty.
    Let us avoid vain quarrelling,
    So that our blood may be spared,
    And may the glorious voice
    Of our race, free from tutelage,
    Rise unitedly, surging as from one man,
    To the dazzling skies above,
    Where its eternal soul, watching over us,
    Brings greatness to the country.

    CHORUS
    Arise, Niger, arise! May our fruitful work
    Rejuvenate the heart of this old continent,
    And may this song resound around the world,
    Like the cry of a just and valiant people.
    Arise, Niger, arise! On land and river,
    To the rhythm of the swelling drum-beats' sound,
    May we ever be united and may each one of us
    Answer the call of this noble future that says to us, 'Forward!'

2. We find again in our children
    All the virtues of our ancestors.
    Such virtues are our inspiration
    For fighting at every moment.
    We confront ferocious and treacherous animals
    Often scarcely armed,
    Seeking to live in dignity,
    Not slaying with a lust to kill.
    In the steppe where all feel thirst,
    In the burning desert,
    Let us march tirelessly forward
    As magnanimous and vigilant masters.

    CHORUS

NIGERIA

Words written collectively

Music by
BENEDICT ELIDE ODIASE (*b.* 1934)
Arr. by W. L. REED

1. A - rise, O com - pa - triots, Ni - ge - ria's call o - bey To serve our Fa - ther - land With love and strength and faith. The la - bour of our he - roes past Shall ne - ver be in

Adopted in 1978.

vain, To serve with heart and might One na - tion bound — in

free - dom, — peace and u - ni - ty.

2. O God of creation,
   Direct our noble cause;
   Guide Thou our leaders right:
   Help our Youth the truth to know,
   In love and honesty to grow,
   And living just and true,
   Great lofty heights attain,
   To build a nation where peace and justice reign.

NORWAY

Words by
BJØRNSTJERNE BJØRNSON (1832 - 1910)

Music by
RIKARD NORDRAAK (1842 - 1866)

Ja, vi el - sker det - te lan - det Som det sti - ger frem,

Fu - ret, vær - bitt o - ver van - net Med de tu - sen hjem.

El - sker, el - sker det og ten - ker På vår far og mor Og den

The words were first published in 1859 and the music probably composed in 1863 or 1864. First performed on 17 May, 1864 to celebrate the 50th anniversary of the Norwegian Constitution. There are eight verses.
Norway also has a Royal Anthem (adopted 1905) with words by Nikolai Fogtmann (1788 - 1815) – the music is by an unknown composer.

sa - ga - natt som sen - ker Drøm - me på vår jord, Og den

sa - ga - natt som sen - ker, Sen - ker drøm - me på vår jord!

2. Norske mann i hus og hytte,
   Takk din store Gud!
   Landet ville han beskytte,
   Skjønt det mørkt så ut.
   Alt, hva fedrene har kjempet,
   Mødrene har grett,
   Har den Herre stille lempet,
   Så vi vant vår rett,
   Har den Herre stille lempet,
   Så vi vant, vi vant vår rett.

3. Ja, vi elsker dette landet,
   Som det stiger frem,
   Furet, værbitt over vannet,
   Med de tusen hjem!
   Og som fedres kamp har hevet
   Det av nød til seir,
   Også vi, når det blir krevet,
   For dets fred slår leir,
   Også vi, nar det blir krevet,
   For dets fred, dets fred slår leir!

Translation by Hilde Midttømme and T. M. Cartledge

1. Yes, we love this country
   Which rises up,
   Rugged and weathered, above the sea,
   With its thousands of homes.
   Love it, love it and think
   About our mothers and fathers
   And the saga of past ages
   That sends dreams to our earth,
   And the saga of past ages
   That sends dreams, sends dreams to our earth.

2. Norsemen, in house and cabin,
   Thank your great God!
   It was His will to protect the country
   Although things looked dark.
   While fathers fought
   And mothers cried,
   Our Lord quietly opened the way
   So that we won our right.
   Our Lord quietly opened the way
   So that we won, we won our right.

3. Yes, we love this country
   Which rises up,
   Rugged and weathered, above the sea,
   With its thousands of homes.
   And as our fathers' struggle has raised it
   From distress to victory,
   We also, when called upon,
   Will strike a blow for its peace.
   We also, when called upon,
   Will strike a blow for its peace, its peace.

OMAN

Words by
RASHID BIN UZAYYIZ AL-KHUSAIDI *

Composer unknown
Arr. by BERNARD EBBINGHAUS

Ya   Rab - ba - na   Eh -

The National Anthem has been in use since 1972.
The new harmonisation dates from 1996.
* Date of birth unknown.

O Lord, protect for us our Majesty the Sultan
And the people of our land,
With honour and peace.

May he live long, strong and supported,
Glorified be his leadership.
For him we shall lay down our lives.
} (twice)

O Oman, since the time of the Prophet
We are a dedicated people amongst the noble Arabs.
Be happy! Qaboos has come
With the blessings of Heaven.

Be cheerful and commend him to the protection of your prayers.

PAKISTAN

Words by
ABU-AL-ASAR HAFEEZ JULLANDHURI (1900 - 1982)

Music by
AHMED GHULAMALI CHAGLA (1902 - 1953)
Arr. by BRYSON GERRARD

Music officially accepted, December 1953. Words officially accepted, August 1954.

hal ja - ne is - taq - bal Say - yai, khu - dae zul ja - lal.

22

Translation

1. Blessed be the sacred land,
   Happy be the bounteous realm,
   Symbol of high resolve,
   Land of Pakistan.
   Blessed be thou citadel of faith.

2. The Order of this Sacred Land
   Is the might of the brotherhood of the people.
   May the nation, the country, and the State
   Shine in glory everlasting.
   Blessed be the goal of our ambition.

3. This flag of the Crescent and the Star
   Leads the way to progress and perfection,
   Interpreter of our past, glory of our present,
   Inspiration of our future,
   Symbol of Almighty's protection.

PALAU

Words by
Several authors

Music by
YMESEI EZEKIEL (1926 - 1984)

Officially adopted on 25 December, 1980.

El ngar cheu - ngel a rir - ch lom - ke - sang.

2. Bo dole ketek a kerruul er a belluad,
   Iolab a blakelreng ma duchelreng.
   Belau a chotil a klengar er kid,
   Mebo dorurtabedul msa klisichel.

3. Bod kai ue reked chim lokiu a reng,
   E dongedmokel radimla koted.
   Lomcheliu a rengedel ma klebkellel,
   Iokiu a budch ma beltikelreng.

4. Dios mo mek ngel tengat ra Be lumam,
   El dimla dikesam ra rechuodelmei.
   Beskemam a klisicham ma llemeltam,
   Iorrurt a klungiolam elmo ch'rechar.

Translation

1. Palau is coming forth with strength and power,
   By her old ways abides still every hour.
   One country, safe, secure, one government
   Under the glowing, floating soft light stands.

2. Let's build our economy's protecting fence
   With courage, faithfulness and diligence.
   Our life is anchored in Palau our land.
   We with our might through life and death defend.

3. In spirit let's join hands, united, one;
   Care for our homeland, from forefathers on.
   Look after its concord, its glory keep.
   Through peace and love and heart's devotion deep.

4. God bless our country, our Island Home always.
   Our sweet inheritance from ancient days.
   Give us the strength and power and all the right
   To govern well to all eternity.

PANAMA
Himno Istmeño
(Isthmus Hymn)

Words by
JERÓNIMO DE LA OSSA (1847 - 1907)

Music by
SANTOS JORGE (1870 - 1941)
Arr. by MARTIN SHAW

CHORUS

Al - can - za - mos por fin la vic-to - ria, En el cam - po fe - liz de la u - nión, Con ar-

Used for the first time on 4 November, 1903, when the people carried the flag of the new Republic through the streets of the capital. It was officially adopted in 1925.

dien - tes ful - go - res de glo - ria Se ilu -

mi - na la nue - va Na - ción, Con ar - dien - tes ful - go - res de

glo - ria Se ilu - mi - na la nue - va Na - ción.

FINE

Meno mosso
p dolce

1. Es pre - ci - so cu - brir con un ve - lo Del pa -

p dolce e legato

423

sa - do el Cal - va - rio y la Cruz,_____ Y que a - dor - ne el a - zul de tu

ciel - o, De con - cor - dia la es - plén - di - da luz. El pro-

gre - so a - ca - ri - cia tus la - res Al com - pás de su - bli - me can-

ción; Ves ru - gir a tus pies am - bos ma - res, Que dan

rum - bo_a   tu no - ble   mi - sión.

D. 𝄇 al Fine

34

2. *En tu suelo cubierto de flores,*
   A los besos del tibio terral,
   Terminaron guerreros fragores,
   Sólo reina el amor fraternal.
   Adelante la pica y la pala,
   Al trabajo sin más dilación:
   Y seremos así prez y gala
   De este mundo feraz de Colón.

   CHORUS

Translation by T. M. Cartledge

CHORUS
We finally attained victory
In the happy field of union.
With glowing splendour,
The new nation is illumined. } (twice)

1. It is necessary to veil with a curtain
   The Calvary and Cross of the past,
   And for you to adorn the azure of your skies
   With the splendid light of concord.
   Progress fondly touches your homes,
   In time with the music of a sublime song.
   You see, roaring at your feet, two oceans
   Which give direction to your noble mission.

   CHORUS

2. On your flower-covered soil,
   Kissed by the warm breeze,
   Warlike clamour has ended
   And only brotherly love reigns.
   Ahead, with spade and stone-mason's hammer!
   To work, without more delay!
   In this way we shall be the honour and glory
   Of this fertile land of Columbus.

   CHORUS

PAPUA NEW GUINEA

Words and music by
THOMAS SHACKLADY (1917 - 2006)
Arr. by KEITH TERRETT

1. O a - rise all you sons of this land, Let us sing of our joy to be free, Prais-ing God and re - joic-ing to be Pa - pu - a New Gui - nea. Shout our

Adopted in 1975.

426

2. Now give thanks to the good Lord above
For His kindness, His wisdom and love
For this land of our fathers so free,
Papua New Guinea.

CHORUS
Shout again for the whole world to hear
Papua New Guinea;
We're independent and we're free,
Papua New Guinea.

PARAGUAY

Words by
FRANCISCO ESTEBAN
ACUÑA DE FIGUEROA (1791 - 1862) *

Music by
FRANCISCO JOSÉ DEBALI (1791 - 1859) †
or FRANCÉS SAUVAGEOT DE DUPUY (1813 - 1861)
or LOUIS CAVEDAGNI (d. 1916) #
Transcribed by
REMBERTO GIMÉNEZ (1899 - 1986)

Adopted in 1846. This present arrangement was declared the official version in May 1934. There are seven verses.
* Francisco Esteban Acuña de Figueroa also wrote the words of the National Anthem of Uraguay.
†Francisco José Debali also composed the music of the National Anthem of Uraguay.
Date of birth unknown.

za - ron el go - rro triun - fal,_____ Y tro-

za - da la au - gus - ta dia - de - ma, E - nal-

CHORUS

za - ron el go - rro triun - fal.

Pa - ra-

Allegro

gua - yos, Re - pú - bli - ca o muer - te! Nue - stro

legato

brí - o nos dió___ li - ber - tad;___ Ni o pre-

so - res, ni sier - vos, a - lien - tan, Don - de

re - i - nan u - nión, e i - gual - dad.___ Ni o pre-

so - res, ni sier - vos, a - lien - tan, Don - de

re - i - nan u - nión e i - gual - dad, u - nión e i - gual -

dad, u - nión e i - gual - dad.

Translation by T. M. Cartledge

VERSE
For three centuries a reign oppressed
The unhappy peoples of America,
But one day, their anger aroused, they said:
"An end to this!" and broke the reign.
Our forefathers, fighting magnificently,
Displayed their martial glory,
And when the august diadem was shattered,
They raised the triumphal cap of liberty.   } (twice)

CHORUS
Paraguayans, Republic or death!
It was our strength that gave us our final liberty.
Neither tyrants nor slaves can continue,
Where unity and equality reign,   } (twice)
Where unity and equality reign.

PERU

Words by
JOSÉ DE LA TORRE UGARTE (1786 - 1831)

Music by
JOSÉ BERNARDO ALZEDO (1788 - 1878)
Arr. by HENRY COLEMAN and W. L. REED

Words and music chosen as result of a competition in 1821. They were declared official on 12 February, 1913. There are six verses.

VERSE

Lar - go tiem - po_el pe - rua - no_o - pri - mi - do La_o - mi-

no - sa ca - de - na_a - rras - tró; _____ Con - de - na - do_a_u - na cruel ser - vi-

dum - bre, Lar - go tiem - po, lar - go tiem - po, lar - go

cresc.

tiem - po en si - len - cio gi - mió.___ Más a - pe - nas el gri - to sa-

gra - do ¡Li - ber - tad! en sus cos - tas___ se o - yó, La jn - do-

len - cia de es - cla - vo sa - cu - de, La hu - mi - lla - da, la hu - mi-

lla - da, la hu - mi - lla - da cer - viz le - van - tó,___ La hu - mi-

lla - da cer - viz___ le-van - tó,   cer - viz___ le - van - tó._____   So - mos

Translation

CHORUS

We are free; let us always be so,
And let the sun rather deny its light
Than that we should fail the solemn vow
Which our country raised to God.

VERSE

For a long time the Peruvian, oppressed,
Dragged the ominous chain;
Condemned to cruel serfdom,
For a long time he moaned in silence.
But as soon as the sacred cry of
Freedom! was heard on his coasts,
He shook off the indolence of the slave,
He raised his humiliated head.

CHORUS

THE PHILIPPINES

Tagalog words by
FELIPE PADILLA DE LEON (1912 - 1992)

Music by
JULIAN FELIPE (1861 - 1944)

Ba - yang ma - gi - liw, Per - las ng Si - la - nga - nan,

A - lab ng pu - so Sa dib - dib mo'y bu - hay.

Lu - pang hi - ni - rang, Du - yan ka ng ma - gi - ting,

First performed in conjunction with the reading of the Act of Proclamation of Independence, 12 June, 1898. The music was composed in 1898, and the original Spanish words were written in 1899 by José Palma (1876 - 1903). Tagalog words officially adopted in 1935.

Sa man-lu-lu-pig Di ka pa-si - si-il. Sa da-gat at bun-dok, Sa si-moy, at sa la-ngit mong bug-haw, May di-lag ang tu-la, At a-wit sa pag-la-yang mi-na-ma-hal. Ang kis-lap ng wa-ta wat

441

mo'y Ta - gum - pay na nag - ni - ning - ning, Ang bi - tu -

in at a - raw niya, Kai - lan pa ma'y di mag - di - di -

lim. Lu - pa ng a - raw ng lu - wal -

ha - tit pag - sin - ta, Bu - hay ay la - ngit sa pi - ling

mo._____ A - ming li ga - ya na pag ma'y

mang - a - a - pi Ang ma - ma - tay nang

da hil sa iyo._____

Translation by T. M. Cartledge from the original Spanish words

Beloved land,
Daughter of the eastern sun,
Your heart is beating
With ardent fire.

Land of love,
Cradle of heroism,
Invaders shall never
Trample on you.

In your blue sky and gentle breezes,
In your mountains and sea,
The epic of your beloved freedom
Shines and throbs.

Your banner, which has illuminated
Victory in battle,
Will never see its stars
Or its sun blotted out.

Land of good fortune, sun and love,
It is sweet to live in your embrace;
It is a glory for your sons
To die for you when you are wronged.

POLAND
Mazurek Dabrowskiego
(Dombrowski's Mazurka)

Words by
JÓZEF WYBICKI (1747 - 1822)

Music by
MICHAL KLEOFAS OGINŚKI (1765 - 1833) *
This is not certain
Arr. by W. L. REED

This song was a favourite with the Polish Legions in the Napoleonic wars. In 1927 it was authorised as its National Anthem by the new Polish republican government.

* The melody resembles that of the National Anthem of Serbia and Montenegro.

Za two-im prze - wo - dem złac - zym się z na - ro - dem.

2. Przejdziem Wisłę, przejdziem Wartę
   Będziem Polakami,
   Dat nam przykład Bonaparte
   Jak zwycięzać mamy.

   CHORUS

3. Jak Czarniecki do Poznania
   Po szwedzkim zaborze,
   Dla ojczyzny ratowania
   Wrócim się przez morze.

   CHORUS

Translation by Jerzy Żebrowski

1. Poland has not yet succumbed.
   As long as we remain,
   What the foe by force has seized,
   Sword in hand we'll gain.

   CHORUS
   March! March, Dąbrowski!
   March from Italy to Poland!
   Under your command
   We shall reach our land.

2. Cross the Vistula and Warta
   And Poles we shall be;
   We've been shown by Bonaparte
   Ways to victory.

   CHORUS

3. As Czarniecki Poznań town regains,
   Fighting with the Swede,
   To free our fatherland from chains,
   We shall return by sea.

   CHORUS

446

PORTUGAL

Words by
HENRIQUE LOPES DE MENDONÇA (1856 - 1931)

Music by
ALFREDO KEIL (1850 - 1907)
Arr. by W. L. REED

First played in January, 1890. Approved as the National Anthem in 1910.

ar - mas! Às ar - mas! Pe-la Pá - tria lu-

tar!_____ Con-tra os ca - nhões mar - char, Mar-char!_____

2. *Desfralda a invicta bandeira*
   À luz viva do teu céu!
   Brade à Europa à terra inteira:
   Portugal não pereceu!
   Beija o solo teu jucundo
   O Oceano a rugir d'amor;
   E o teu braço vencedor
   Deu novos mundos ao mundo!

   CHORUS

3. *Saudai o sol que desponta*
   Sobre um ridente porvir;
   Seja o eco de uma afronta
   O sinal do ressurgir.
   Ráios dessa aurora forte
   São como beijos de mãe
   Que nos guardam, nos sustêm
   Contra as injúrias da sorte.

   CHORUS

Translation

1. Heroes of the sea, noble race,
   Valiant and immortal nation,
   Now is the hour to raise up on high once more
   Portugal's splendour.
   From out of the mists of memory,
   Oh Homeland, we hear the voices
   Of your great forefathers
   That shall lead you on to victory!

   CHORUS
   To arms, to arms
   On land and sea!
   To arms, to arms
   To fight for our Homeland!
   To march against the enemy guns!

2. Unfurl the unconquerable flag
   In the bright light of your sky!
   Cry out to all Europe and the whole world
   That Portugal has not perished.
   Your happy land is kissed
   By the Ocean that murmurs with love.
   And your conquering arm
   Has given new worlds to the world!

   CHORUS

3. Salute the Sun that rises
   On a smiling future:
   Let the echo of an insult be
   The signal for our revival.
   The rays of that powerful dawn
   Are like a mother's kisses
   That protect us and support us
   Against the insults of fate.

   CHORUS

QATAR

Words by
SHEIKH MUBARAK BIN SAIF AL-THANI (*b.* 1953)

Music by
ABDUL AZIZ NASSER (*b.* 1952)
Arr. by W. L. REED

Adopted 7 December, 1996.

D. 𝄋 al Fine

Kasamn bimn rafaa asama kasamn bimn nashara adia
Qataron satabko huratn tasmu biroha alaawfia
Siru ala nahji alaali wa ala dia alaambia
Qataron bikalbi siratum izum wa amjad alaaba
Qataru arrijali alaawalina humatuna yawma annida
Wa hama imu yawma salam jawarihu yawma alfida.

Translation

I swear by the one who raised the sky
I swear by the one who spread the light
Qatar shall forever be free
Exalted by the spirit of the allegiants
Track the footsteps of forefathers
And the glow of apostles
Qatar my whole way of life
The grandeur and glory of pride
Qatar the homeland of ancestors
Our champions on the day of sacrifice
Doves in time of peace
Predators on day of war.

ROMANIA

Words by
ANDREI MUREŞANU (1816 - 1863)

Music by
ANTON PANN (1796 - 1854)

Adopted in April, 1990.

cum ori nici - o - da - tă cro - ieş te-ţi al - tă

soar - tă, La ca - re să se-n - chi - ne şi

cru - zii tăi duş - mani, şi cru - zii tăi duş -

mani! A - cum ori nici - o - da tă cro -
ieş te-ţi al - tă soar - tă, La ca - re să se-n -
chi - ne şi cru - zii tăi duş - mani, şi

cru - zii— tăi   duş - mani!   mînt!

2. *Acum ori niciodată să dăm dovezi la lume*
   Că-n aste mîini mai curge un sînge de roman
   Și că-n a noastre piepturi păstrăm cu fală-un nume
   Triumfător în lupte, un nume de Traian!

3. *Priviți mărețe umbre, Mihai, Ștefan, Corvine,*
   Româna națiune, ai voștri strănepoți,
   Cu brațele armate, cu focul vostru-n vine,
   „Viața-n libertate ori moarte !" strigăm toți.

4. *Preoți cu crucea-n frunte! Căci oastea e creștină,*
   Deviza-i libertate și scopul ei prea sfînt,
   Murim mai bine-n luptă, cu glorie deplină,
   Decît să fim sclavi iarăși în vechiul nost pămînt!

Translation by Gabriel Gafita

1. Wake up, Romanian, from your deadly slumber,
   In which barbaric tyrants kept you so long by force!
   Now or never is the time for you to have a new fate,
   Which should command respect of even your cruel enemies.

2. Now or never is the time for us to prove to the entire world
   That in these arms a Roman blood still flows,
   And that in our hearts we proudly keep a name
   Triumphant in all battles, the name of Trajan.*

3. Behold, glorious shadows, Mihai, Stephen, Corvin,†
   That is the Romanian nation, your own great-grandsons,
   With weapons in their hands, your fire in their veins,
   All shouting, "We want to live in freedom, or else better die!"

4. Priests carry the cross ahead! The army is all Christian,
   Its banner is called freedom and its ideal is sacred,
   We'd rather die in battle, and do it in full glory,
   Than live again like slaves in our dear old land.

* Roman emperor who conquered Dacia in 106 A.D.
† Romanian princes of the three Romanian principalities, Walachia, Moldavia and Transylvania, in the 15th and 16th centuries.

457

RUSSIAN FEDERATION

Words by
SERGEI VLADIMIROVICH MIKHALKOV (*b.* 1913)

Music by
ALEXANDR VASILIEVICH ALEXANDROV
(1883 - 1946)

Originally adopted as the Soviet National anthem in 1943, replaced in 1991 and restored in 2001 together with new words.

1. *Rossiya svyaschennaya nasha dyerzhava!*
   Rossiya lyubimaya nasha strana!
   Moguchaya volya, vyelikaya slava
   Tvoyo dostoyan'ye na vsya vryemyena.

   CHORUS
   Slav'sya, Otechestvo nashe svobodnoye
   Bratskikh narodov soyuz vyekovoy,
   Predkami dannaya mudrost' narodnaya
   Slav'sya strana! My gordimsya toboy!

2. *Ot yuzhnykh morey do polyarnogo kraya*
   Raskmulis' nashi lesa i polya.
   Odna ty na svete! Odna ty takaya!
   Khranimaya bogom rodnaya zyemlya.

   CHORUS

3. *Shirokiy prostor dlya mechty i dlya zhizni*
   Gryaduschiye nam otkryvayut goda.
   Nam silu dayot nasha vernost' otchiznye.
   Tak bylo, tak yest', i tak budet vsyegda!

   CHORUS

Translation by Fabio Lazzati

1. Russia, you are our sacred Power!
   Russia, you are our beloved land!
   The mighty will and the immense glory –
   Here is your heritage in any predicament.

   CHORUS
   Glory be to you, free fatherland of ours –
   Everlasting alliance of fraternal peoples,
   Popular wisdom handed on by the forefathers,
   Glory be to you, land of ours! We are proud of you!

2. Our woods and our fields extend
   From the southern seas as far as the North Pole.
   You are a one in the world! You are quite a one,
   Native land protected by God.

   CHORUS

3. To us the years to come open wide
   Boundless spaces to dream and life.
   Our allegiance to the fatherland gives us strength.
   So it was, so it is and so it will ever be.

   CHORUS

RWANDA

Words by
FAUSTIN MURIGO *

Music by
JEAN-BOSC HASHAKAIMANA †
Arr. by MARTIN WEHN

Rw - anda nzi - za Gi - hu - gu cya - cu, Wu - je imi - so - zi, i - bi - ya - ga n'i - bi - ru - nga. Ngo - byi idu - he - tse, ga - ho - ra - ne i-shya. Re - ka tu - ku - ra - te tu-

Adopted in 2001.
* Year of birth unknown.
† Year of birth unknown.

2. *Horana imana murage mwiza*
   Ibyo tugukesha ntibishyikirwa
   Umuco dusangiye uraturanga
   Ururimi rwacu rukaduhuza
   Uwenge, umutima, amaboko yacu
   Nibigukungahaze bikwiye
   Uhore utera imbere ubutitsa.

3. *Abakurambere b'intwari*
   Bitanze batizigama
   Baraguhanga uvamo ubukombe
   Utsinda ubukoroni na mpatsibihugu
   Byayogoje Afurika yose
   None uganje mu bwigenge
   Tubukomeyeho ubuziraherezo.

4. *Komeza imihigo Rwanda dukunda*
   Duhagurukiye kukwitangira
   Ngo amahoro asabe mu bagutuye
   Wishyire wizane muri byose
   Urangwe n'ishyaka utere imbere
   Uhamye umubano n'amahanga yose
   Maze ijabo ryawe riguhe ijambo.

French version

1. *Rwanda, notre beau et cher pays*
    Paré de collines, de lacs et de volcans
    Mère-patrie, sois toujours comblée de bonheur
    Nous tous tes enfants: Abanyarwanda
    Chantons ton éclat et proclamons tes hauts faits
    Toi, Giron maternel de nous tous
    Sois à jamais admiré, prospère et couvert d'éloges.

2. *Précieux héritage, que Dieu te protège*
    Tu nous as comblé de biens inestimables
    Notre culture commune nous identifie
    Notre unique langue nous unifie
    Que notre intelligence, notre conscience et nos forces
    Te comblent de richesses diversifiées
    Pour un développement sans cesse renouvelé.

3. *Nos valeureux aïeux*
    Se sont donnés corps et âmes
    Jusqu'à faire de toi une grande Nation
    Tu as eu raison du joug colonialo-impérialiste
    Qui a dévasté l'Afrique tout entière
    Et te voici aise de ton independance souveraine
    Acquis que sans cesse nous défendrons.

4. *Maintiens ce cap, Rwanda bien-aimé*
    Debout nous nous engageons pour toi
    Afin que la paix règne dans tout le pays
    Que tu sois libre de toute entrave
    Que ta détermination engage le progrès
    Qu'excellent tes relations avec tous les pays
    Et qu'enfin ta fierté te vaille estime.

Translation by K. Jonathan Fryer

1   Rwanda, our beautiful and dear country
    Adorned with hills, lakes and volcanoes
    Motherland, be always filled with good fortune
    We, all your children : Abanyarwande
    Sing of your brilliance and proclaim your fine deeds
    You, maternal bosom of us all
    Be forever admired, prosperous and covered in praise.

2   Precious heritage, may God protect you
    You have provided us with priceless things
    Our common culture identifies us
    Our language unifies us
    May our intelligence, our conscience and our efforts
    Fill you with diverse riches
    For ever continuing development.

3   Our gallant ancestors
    Gave body and soul
    To make you a great nation
    You have come from the colonial, imperialist yoke
    Which devastated the whole of Africa
    And here you are, comfortable with your sovereign independance
    Whose acquisition we shall defend unceasingly.

4   Keep this course, beloved Rwanda
    We stand and pledge ourselves for you
    So that peace reigns throughout the country
    May you be free from shackles
    May you embrace progress with determination
    And have excellent relations with every country
    And finally be proud of your worth.

SAINT KITTS AND NEVIS

Words and music by
KENRICK ANDERSON GEORGES (*b*. 1955)
Arr. by W. L. REED

Maestoso

1. O Land of Beau - ty! Our

coun - try where peace a-bounds, Thy chil - dren stand___
just - ice and li - ber - ty, With wis - dom and___

free On the strength of will and love. With
truth We will serve and hon - our thee. No

Adopted in 1983.

467

God   in all our strug - gles, Saint   Kitts   and Ne - vis
sword   nor spear can con - quer, For   God   will sure de -

be   A   Na -   tion bound to - ge -   ther   With a
fend.   His   bless -   ings shall for e -   ver   To pos -

FINE   *D. ％ al Fine*

com - mon des - ti - ny.   2. As stal - warts we stand,   For
ter - i - ty   ex - tend.

468

SAINT LUCIA

Words by
CHARLES JESSE (1897 - 1985)

Music by
LETON FELIX THOMAS (*b.* 1926)
Arr. by W. L. REED

1. Sons and daugh-ters of Saint Lu - cia, Love the land that gave us birth, Land of bea - ches, hills and val - leys, Fair - est isle of __ all the earth. Where - so-ev - er

Originally adopted in 1967 on achieving Statehood, and again in 1979 when becoming independent.

you may roam,— Love, oh— love our is - land home!

2. Gone the times when nations battled
   For this 'Helen of the West',
   Gone the days when strife and discord
   Dimmed her children's toil and rest.
   Dawns at last a brighter day,
   Stretches out a glad new way.

3. May the good Lord bless our island,
   Guard her sons from woe and harm!
   May our people live united,
   Strong in soul and strong in arm!
   Justice, Truth and Charity,
   Our ideal for ever be!

SAINT VINCENT and THE GRENADINES

Words by
PHYLLIS JOYCE McCLEAN PUNNETT (1917 - 2004)

Music by
JOEL BERTRAM MIGUEL (*b.* 1938)
Arr. by W. L. REED

Maestoso

1. Saint Vin - cent! Land so beau - ti - ful, With joy - ful hearts we pledge to thee Our loy - al - ty and love, and vow To keep you e - ver free.

CHORUS

What - e'er the fu - ture brings, Our

Originally adopted in 1969 on achieving Statehood, and again in 1979 when becoming independent.

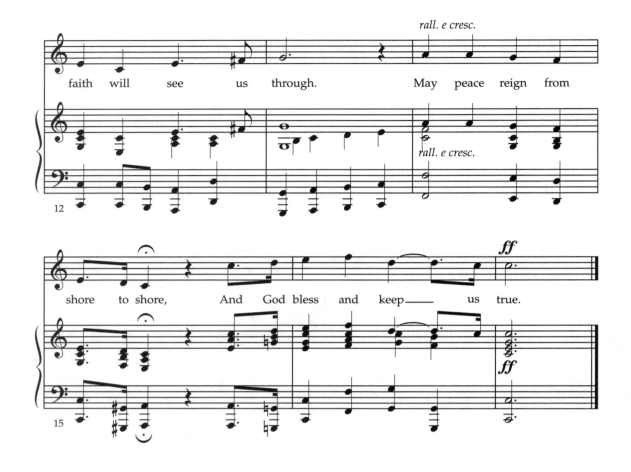

faith will see us through. May peace reign from shore to shore, And God bless and keep us true.

2. Hairoun! Our fair and blessed Isle,
   Your mountains high, so clear and green,
   Are home to me, though I may stray,
   A haven, calm, serene.

   CHORUS

3. Our little sister islands are
   Those gems, the lovely Grenadines,
   Upon their seas and golden sands
   The sunshine ever beams.

   CHORUS

472

SAMOA
The Banner of Freedom

Words and music by
SAUNI IIGA KURESA (1900 - 1978)
Arr. by HENRY COLEMAN

Sa - moa, tu - la'i ma si - si ia lau fu'a, lou pa - le le - a; Sa - moa, tu - la'i ma si - si ia lau fu'a, lou pa - le - le - a; { Va - / Pu -

On 1 January, 1962 Western Samoa became the first sovereign independent Polynesian State. Selected by the Council of the Committee to be the National Anthem, it was sung as the flag of the Western Samoan Government was raised. In 1997 it was decided to drop the word Western.

Translation

Samoa, arise and raise your banner that is your crown!
Oh! see and behold the stars on the waving banner!
They are a sign that Samoa is able to lead.
Oh! Samoa, hold fast
Your freedom for ever!
Do not be afraid; as you are founded on God;
Our treasured precious liberty.
Samoa, arise and wave
Your banner that is your crown!

SAN MARINO

Words by
GIOSUÉ CARDUCCI (1835 - 1907) *

Music by
FEDERICO CONSOLO (1841 - 1906) †

O - no - re a te o - no - re o an - ti - ca Re -
pu - bli - ca vir - tuo - - - sa tuo - - - sa
ge - ne - ro - - - sa fi - den - te o - no - re a

Adopted in 1894.

* Unofficial words.

† The music is based on a tenth century chorale from a breviary in the *Biblioteca Laurenziana*.

Free Translation

Honour to you, O ancient Republic,
Virtuous, generous, faithful!
Honour to you, and live eternally
Within the life and the glory of Italy.

SÃO TOMÉ and PRÍNCIPE

Words by
ALDA NEVES DA GRAÇA
DO ESPIRITO SANTO (*b.* 1926)

Music by
MANUEL DOS SANTOS BARRETO
DE SOUSA E ALMEIDA (*b.* 1933)
Arr. by W. L. REED

Adopted in 1975.

CHORUS
Independência total,
Glorioso canto do povo,
Independência total,
Hino sagrado de combate.
Dinamismo
Na luta nacional,
Juramento eterno
No país soberano de São Tomé e Príncipe.

1. *Guerrilheiro da guerra sem armas na mão,*
   Chama viva na alma do povo,
   Congregando os filhos das ilhas
   Em redor da Pátria Imortal.

2. *Independência total, total e completa,*
   Construindo, no progresso e na paz,
   A nação mais ditosa da Terra,
   Com os braços heróicos do povo.

CHORUS
Independência total,
Glorioso canto do povo.
Independência total,
Hino sagrado de combate.

3. *Trabalhando, lutando, lutando e vencendo,*
   Caminhamos a passos gigantes
   Na cruzada dos povos africanos,
   Hasteando a bandeira nacional.

4. *Voz do povo, presente, presente em conjunto,*
   Vibra rijo no coro da esperança
   Ser herói no hora do perigo,
   Ser herói no ressurgir do País.

CHORUS
Independência total,
Glorioso canto do povo,
Independência total,
Hino sagrado de combate.
Dinamismo
Na luta nacional,
Juramento eterno
No pais soberano de São Tomé e Príncipe.

Translation by T. M. Cartledge

CHORUS
Total independence,
Glorious song of the people,
Total independence,
Sacred hymn of combat.
Dynamism
In the national struggle,
Eternal oath
To the sovereign country of São Tomé and Pr ncipe.

1. Warriors in the war without weapons,
   Live flame in the soul of the people,
   Congregating the sons of the islands
   Around the Immortal Fatherland.

2. Total independence, total and complete,
   Building, in progress and peace,
   With the heroic hands of the people,
   The happiest nation on earth.

CHORUS (first 4 lines only)

3. Working, struggling, struggling and conquering,
   We go ahead with giant steps
   In the crusade of the African peoples,
   Raising the national flag.

4. Voice of the people, present, present and united,
   Strong beat in the heart of hope
   To be a hero in the hour of peril,
   A hero of the Nation's resurgence.

CHORUS (as at beginning)

480

SAUDI ARABIA

Words by
IBRAHIM KHAFAJI (*b.* 1935)

Music by
ABDUL RAHMAN AL-KHATEEB (*b.* 1923)
Arr. by W. L. REED

Sa - re - i___ Lil Ma - jd Wal - al - ya Maj - je - di Le Kha - leg As - sa-

ma

ma

War - fai El Khaf - fag___ Akh - dar

Yah - mil An - noor al mo - sat - tar Rad - de - dy Al - lah___ Wak - bar

First performed in 1947, adopted in 1950.

Translation by M. A. S. Abdul Haleem

Hasten to glory and supremacy!
Glorify the Creator of the heavens
And raise the green, fluttering flag,
Carrying the emblem of Light!
Repeat - God is greatest!
O my country,
My country, may you always live,
The glory of all Muslims!
Long live the King,
For the flag and the country!

SCOTLAND
Flower of Scotland

Words and music by
ROY WILLIAMSON (1936 - 1990)
Arr. by RONNIE BROWN

1. Oh Flower of Scot - land When will we see yer like a - gain. That fou-ght and died for yer

Adopted in 1997.

lost now Which those so de-ar-ly held That stood____ a-

gainst him Proud Ed-ward's Ar — my And se-nt him

ho-me-ward tae think____ a-gain. 3. Those days are

passed now and in the past____ they must re-

main

But we can still rise now

And

be the Na - tion a - gain That stood a - gainst him

Proud Ed - ward's Ar - my

And se - nt him

ho - me - ward

tae think a - gain.

4. Oh Flower of Scot - land When will we see___ yer like a -

gain That fou - ght and died for Yer

wee bit hi - ll and glen And stood___ a - gainst him proud Ed - ward's

Ar - my And se - nt him ho - me-ward tae think___ a -

gain.

rall.

SÉNÉGAL

Words by
LÉOPOLD SÉDAR SENGHOR (1906 - 2001)

Music by
HERBERT PEPPER (1912 - 2001) *

1. Pin - cez tous vos Ko - ras‡ Frap - pez les ba - la - fons, Le Lion rouge a ru - gi Le Domp - teur de la brousse d'un

Adopted in 1960.

* Herbert Pepper also wrote the music for the National Anthem of the Central African Republic.

† The Kora is the harp-lute of the Sénégalese Griots.

bond s'est é - lan - cé Dis - si - pant les tén - è - bres. So -

leil sur nos ter - reurs, So - leil sur nos es - poirs.

De - bout frè - res, voi - ci l'A - fri - que ras - sem - blé - e.

CHORUS

Fi - bres de mon cœur vert, E - pau - le contre é - pau - le,

Mes plus que frères O Sé - né - ga - lais, de - bout!____

U - nis - sons la mer et les sour - ces, U - nis - sons la steppe et la fo - rêt. Sa -

1. lut Af - ri - que mè - re.

2. lut A - fri - que mère.

2. *Sénégal, toi le fils de l'écume du Lion,*
   Toi surgi de la nuit au galop des chevaux,
   Rends-nous, oh! rends-nous l'honneur de nos Ancêtres,
   Splendides comme ébène et forts comme le muscle
   Nous disons droits - l'épée n'a pas une bavure.

   CHORUS

3. *Sénégal, nous faisons nôtre ton grand dessein:*
   Rassembler les poussins à l'abri des milans
   Pour en faire, de l'Est à l'Ouest, du Nord au Sud,
   Dressé, un même peuple, un peuple sans couture
   Mais un peuple tourné vers tous les vents du monde.

   CHORUS

4. *Sénégal, comme toi, comme tous nos héros,*
   Nous serons durs sans haine et des deux bras ouverts.
   L'épée, nous la mettrons dans la paix du fourreau,
   Car le travail sera notre arme et la parole.
   Le Bantou est un frère, et l'Arabe et le Blanc.

   CHORUS

5. *Mais que si l'ennemi incendie nos frontières*
   Nous serons tous dressés et les armes au poing:
   Un Peuple dans sa foi défiant tous les malheurs,
   Les jeunes et les vieux, les hommes et les femmes.
   La Mort, oui! Nous disons la Mort, mais pas la honte.

   CHORUS

1. Sound, all of you, your Koras,
   Beat the drums,
   The red Lion has roared,
   The Tamer of the bush with one leap has rushed forward
   Scattering the gloom.
   Light on our terrors,
   Light on our hopes.
   Arise, brothers, Africa behold united!

   CHORUS
   Shoulder to shoulder,
   O people of Sénégal, more than brothers to me, arise!
   Unite the sea and the springs,
   Unite the steppe and the forest!
   Hail, mother Africa,
   Hail, mother Africa!

2. Sénégal, thou son of the Lion
   Arise in the night with great speed,
   Restore, oh, restore to us the honour of our ancestors,
   Magnificent as ebony and strong as muscles!
   We are a straight people - the sword has no fault.

   CHORUS

3. Sénégal, we make your great design our own:
   To gather the chicks, sheltering them from kites,
   To make from them, from East to West, from North to South,
   A people rising as one, in seamless unity,
   Yet a people facing all the winds of the earth.

   CHORUS

4. Sénégal, like thee, like all our heroes,
   We will be stern without hatred, and with open arms.
   The sword we will put peacefully in its sheath,
   For work and words will be our weapon.
   The Bantu is our brother, the Arab, and the White man too.

   CHORUS

5. But if the enemy violates our frontiers,
   We will all be ready, weapons in our hands;
   A people in its faith defying all evil;
   Young and old, men and women,
   Death, yes! but not dishonour.

   CHORUS

SERBIA AND MONTENEGRO

Words by
SAMUEL TOMAŠIK (1813 - 1887)

Composer unknown *
Arr. by BORIVOJE SIMIĆ

1. Hej Slo - ve - ni, jŏ - ste ži - vi— Reč na - ših de -
do - va, Dok za na - rod sr - ce bi - je— Nji - ho - vih si -
no - ra. Ži - vi, ži - vi duh slo - ven - ski,

This became the National Anthem of Yugoslavia in 1945, and was retained by Serbia and Montenegro after the breakup of the former Yugoslavia. In May 2006 a referendum was held in Montenegro and there was a majority vote for independence.
* The melody resembles that of the National Anthem of Poland.

Ži - ve - će ve - kov' - ma,   Za - lud pre - ti— po - nor pa - kla,—

Za - lud va - tra gro - ma,   Za - lud va - tra gro - ma!

Translation

2. *Nek se sada i nad nama*
Burom sve raznese,
Stena puca, dub se lama,
Zemlja nek se trese.
Mi stojimo postojano
Kano klisurine;
Proklet bio izdajica ⎫
Svoje domovine! ⎭ (twice)

1. Hey Slavs! our grandfathers' word still lives,
   As long as their sons' heart beats for the people.
   It lives, the spirit of Slavs lives, it will live for centuries,
   The abyss of hell threatens in vain, the fire of thunder is in vain.

2. Now let everything above us be carried away by the bura.*
   The rock cracks, the oak breaks, let the ground shake.
   We stand steadfastly like cliffs;
   Let the traitor of his homeland be damned!

*A fast and sudden north-east wind, which blows along the eastern Adriatic coast.

SEYCHELLES
Koste Seselwa
(Seychellois, Unite!)

Words and music by
DAVID FRANÇOIS MARC ANDRÉ (*b.* 1958)
and GEORGE CHARLES ROBERT PAYET (*b.* 1959)
Arr. by W. L. REED

Officially adopted on 18 June, 1996, replacing the former National Anthem.

dye._____ Pre - zerv la - bo - té nou pe - i_____ La - ri -

ses nou lo - se - an._____ En le - ri - taz byen

pre - sye Pour bo - ner nou zan - fan. Res - ter tou -

zour dan li - ni - té Fer mon - te nou pa - vi - yon.

An - sanm pour tou le-ter-ni-té, Kos - te Se - sel - wa.

Translation

Seychelles, our homeland.
Where we live in harmony.
Joy, love and peace,
We thank God.
Let us preserve the beauty of our country
And the wealth of our oceans,
Which are both precious heritages
For the future of our children.
Let us stay in unity always
Under the colours of our new flag,
And together for eternity,
Seychellois, Unite!

SIERRA LEONE

Words by
CLIFFORD NELSON FYLE (1933 - 2006)

Music by
JOHN JOSEPH AKAR (1927 - 1975)
Arr. by HENRY COLEMAN

Maestoso

1. High we ex - alt— thee, realm of the free; Great is the love— we

have for— thee; Firm - ly u - nit - ed e - ver we stand,

Sing - ing thy praise,— O— nat - ive— land. We raise up our hearts and our

Adopted on 27 April, 1961.

2. One with a faith that wisdom inspires,
   One with a zeal that never tires;
   Ever we seek to honour thy name,
   Ours is the labour, thine the fame.
   We pray that no harm on thy children may fall,
   That blessing and peace may descend on us all;
   So may we serve thee ever alone,
   Land that we love, our Sierra Leone.

3. Knowledge and truth our forefathers spread,
   Mighty the nations whom they led;
   Mighty they made thee, so too may we
   Show forth the good that is ever in thee.
   We pledge our devotion, our strength and our might,
   Thy cause to defend and to stand for thy right;
   All that we have be ever thine own,
   Land that we love, our Sierra Leone.

SINGAPORE

Majulah Singapura
(May Singapore Progress)

Words and music by
ZUBIR SAID (1907 - 1987)
Arr. by HENRY COLEMAN

For Royal Salute, play from * to *.

First performed in September, 1958. It became very popular and when the country became self-governing on 3 June, 1959, it was decided to make it the National Anthem and was officially adopted on 30 November, 1959.

Translation

Let us, the people of Singapore, together march forward towards happiness.
Our noble aspiration is to see Singapore achieve success.
Let us unite in a new spirit.
We all pray: 'May Singapore Progress', 'May Singapore Progress'.

SLOVAKIA

Words by
JANKO MATÚŠKA (1821 - 1877)

Composer unknown *

Allegro energico (♩ = 84)

1. Nad Ta - trou sa blý - ska, hro - my di - vo bi - jú,

nad Ta - trou sa blý - ska, hro - my di - vo bi - jú.

Za - stav - me sa, bra - tia, ved' sa o - ny stra - tia,

* The melody is a Slovak folksong commemorating the exodus of Slovak students from Bratislava in 1843.
On separating from Czechoslovakia on 1 January, 1993, Slovakia retained her section of the former National Anthem as her National Anthem.

2. To Slovensko naše posial' tvrdo spalo,
   To Slovensko naše posial' tvrdo spalo.
   Ale blesky hromu zbudzujú ho k tomu, aby sa prebralo.
   Ale blesky hromu zbudzujú ho k tomu, aby sa prebralo.

Translation

1. Lightning flashes over the Tatra, the thunder pounds wildly,
   Lightning flashes over the Tatra, the thunder pounds wildly,
   Let us pause, brothers, they will surely disappear, the Slovaks will revive,
   Let us pause, brothers, they will surely disappear, the Slovaks will revive.

2. This Slovakia of ours has been fast asleep until now,
   This Slovakia of ours has been fast asleep until now.
   But the thunder and lightning are encouraging it to come alive,
   But the thunder and lightning are encouraging it to come alive.

SLOVENIA
Zdravljica
(A Toast)

Words by
FRANCE PREŠEREN (1800 - 1849)

Music by
STANKO PREMRL (1880 - 1965)
Arr. by W. L. REED

Ži - ve naj vsi na-ro-di, ki hre-pe-ne do-ča-kat dan, Da ko-der son-ce ho-di, pre-pir iz sve-ta bo pre-gnan, Da ro-jak prost bo vsak, ne vrag, le so-sed

Adopted officially on 29 March, 1990.
There are eight verses in all, but only the seventh verse is sung.

bo me - jak, Da ro - jak, prost bo vsak, ne vrag, le so - sed

bo, _____ Ne vrag, le so - sed bo me - jak!

Translation

God's blessing on all nations,
Who long and work for that bright day,
When o'er earth's habitations
No war, no strife shall hold its sway;
Who long to see
That all men free
No more shall foes, but neighbours be.

SOLOMON ISLANDS

Words by
PANAPASA BALEKANA (*b.* 1929)
and MATILA BALEKANA (*b.* 1932)

Music by
PANAPASA BALEKANA (*b.* 1929)

Chosen as a result of a competition, and first sung on Independence Day, 7 July, 1978.

SOMALIA

Author unknown

Composer unknown
Arr. by FABIO LAZZATI

Translation

Somaliyaay toosoo
Toosoo isku tiirsada ee
Hadba kiina taag daranee
Taageera waligiinee.

Somalia wake up,
Wake up and join hands together
And we must help the weakest of our people
All of the time.

Adopted in 2000.

SOUTH AFRICA

Words by
ENOCH MANKAYI SONTONGA (1860 - 1904) and
CORNELIS JACOB LANGENHOVEN (1873 - 1932)

Music by
ENOCH MANKAYI SONTONGA (1860 - 1904) and
MARTHINUS LOURENS DE VILLIERS (1885 - 1977)

With effect from 27 April 1994 South Africa adopted two official National Anthems, 'The Call of South Africa' and 'Nkosi Sikelel' iAfrika'. In May 1995, with Cabinet approval, the National Anthems were shortened and merged into one version for ceremonial purposes. The new version begins with the Nguni and Sotho versions of 'Nkosi Sikelel' iAfrika', continues with the opening lines of 'Die Stem van Suid-Afrika' and ends with an excerpt from the English verison of 'The Call of South Africa'.

Translation

(Xhosa and Zulu)
God bless Africa,
Lift her horn on high,
Hear our prayers.
God bless us
Who are Your people.

(Sotho)
God save our nation,
End wars and strife.
South Africa.

(Afrikaans)
Ringing out from our blue heavens, from our deep seas breaking round;
Over everlasting mountains where the echoing crags resound.

SPAIN
Marcha Real
(Royal March)

No words*

Composer unknown†
Arr. by W. L. REED

Marziale marcato e sostenuto

† The *Marcha Real* dates from 3 September, 1770, when it was declared by Royal Decree of Carlos III as the Spanish Royal March. In July 1942 General Franco issued a decree declaring it as the National Anthem.
* There are no official words, though two writers, Eduardo Marquina (1879 - 1946) and José Mar a Pemán y Pemart n (1897 - 1981), have written verses at different times.

SRI LANKA

Sinhalese words by
ANANDA SAMARAKONE (1911 - 1962)
Author of Tamil words unknown

Music by
ANANDA SAMARAKONE (1911 - 1962)
Arr. by SURYA SENA

Adopted in 1952. There are two additional verses in which the melody is slightly varied.

Translation

Mother Lanka – we salute Thee!
Plenteous in prosperity, Thou,
Beauteous in grace and love,
Laden with corn and luscious fruit
And fragrant flowers of radiant hue,
Giver of life and all good things,
Our land of joy and victory,
Receive our grateful praise sublime,
Lanka! we worship Thee.

SUDAN

Words by
SAYED AHMAD MUHAMMAD SALIH (1896 - 1971)

Music by
AHMAD MURJAN (1905 - 1974)
Arr. by T. M. CARTLEDGE

Lyrics:
Nah - nu — Djun - dul - lah Djun - dul - wa - tan.
In — Da A Da Il Fi - da Lam Na - khun.
Na - ta - had - dal Maut End - al - mi - han.

Officially adopted in 1956.

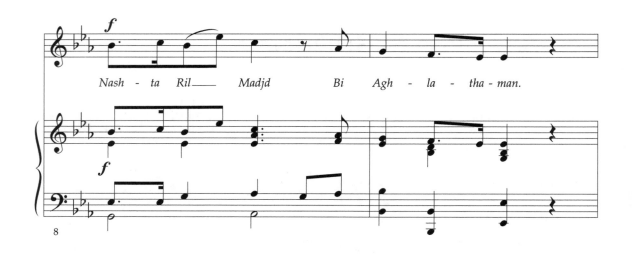

Nash - ta Ril— Madjd Bi Agh - la - tha - man.

Ha - thi - hil Ard La - na! Fal - ya - ish Su - da - nu - na,

A - la - man Bayn Al U - mam.

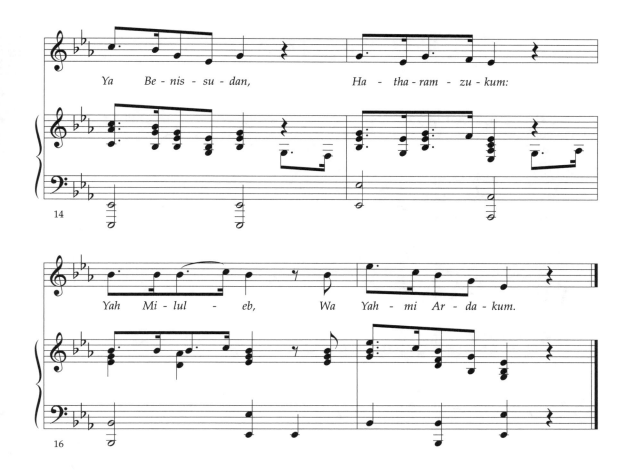

Ya Be - nis - su - dan, Ha - tha - ram - zu - kum:

Yah Mi - lul - eb, Wa Yah - mi Ar - da - kum.

Translation by T. M. Cartledge

We are the army of God and of our land,
We shall never fail when called to sacrifice.
Whether braving death, hardship or pain,
We give our lives as the price of glory.
May this our land, Sudan, live long,
Showing all nations the way.
Sons of the Sudan, summoned now to serve,
Shoulder the task of preserving our country.

SURINAM

Dutch words by
CORNELIS ATSES HOEKSTRA (1852 - 1911)
Sranan words by
HENRY DE ZIEL (1916 - 1975)

Music by
JOHANNES CORSTIANUS DE PUY (1835 - 1924)
Arr. by HENRY COLEMAN

The music was written in 1876, the words in 1893. Officially adopted on 7 December, 1954.

Translation by T. M. Cartledge
(from the Dutch)

God be with our Surinam!
May He glorify our beautiful land!
However we came together here,
We are pledged to your soil.
As we work, let us remember
That justice and truth make us free.
Practising all that is good
Will make our country a worthy land.

SWAZILAND

Words by
ANDREASE ENOKE FANYANA SIMELANE (*b.* 1934)

Music by
DAVID KENNETH RYCROFT (1924 - 1997)

Adopted on 6 September, 1968

Translation

O Lord our God, bestower of all blessings on the Swazi;
We give Thee thanks for all our good fortune,
We offer thanks and praise for our King
And for our fair land, its hills and rivers.
Thy blessing be on all rulers of our Country;
Might and power are Thine alone;
We pray Thee to grant us wisdom
Without deceit or malice,
Establish and fortify us,
Lord eternal.

SWEDEN
Sång Till Norden
(Song of the North)

Words by
RICHARD DYBECK (1811 - 1877)

Composer unknown *
Arr. by EDVIN KALLSTENIUS

* First sung in 1844 with the title 'Sång till Norden' (Song of the North); its use as a National Anthem dates from 1880 - 1890.
Sweden also has a Royal Anthem (adopted 1893) with words by Carl Wilhelm August Strandberg (1818 - 1877) and
music by Otto Lindblad (1809 - 1864).

2. *Du tronar på minnen från fornstora da'r,*
   Då ärat ditt namn flög över jorden.
   Jag vet att du är och du blir, vad du var,
   Ja, jag vill leva, jag vill dö i Norden. } (twice)

Translation by T. M. Cartledge

1. You ancient, free and mountainous North,
   Of quiet, joyful beauty,
   I greet you, loveliest land on earth,
   Your sun, your sky, your green meadows. } (twice)

2. You are throned on memories of olden days
   When the honour of your name spread over the earth.
   I know that you are and will remain what you were.
   Oh, may I live, may I die in the Nordic North! } (twice)

SWITZERLAND
Swiss Psalm

Words
German words by LEONHARD WIDMER (1808 - 1868)
French words by CHARLES CHATELANAT (1833 - 1907)
Italian words by CAMILLO VALSANGIACOMO (1898 - 1978)
Surselvish words by ALFONS TUOR (1871 - 1904)
Ladinish words by GION ANTONI BÜHLER (1825 - 1897)

Music by
ALBERICH ZWYSSIG (1808 -1854)
Arr. by OTTO KREIS

The original version dates from 1841. Adopted as the official National Anthem in 1961.

531

Wenn der Al - pen Firn sich rö - tet,
Les beau - tés de la pa - tri - e
Nel tri - pu - dio del mat - ti - no
Cu las bri - schan dall' au - ro - ra,
Cur ils munts stra - glu - schan su - ra,

Be - tet, frei - e Schwei - zer, be - tet!
Par - lent à l'âme at - ten - dri - e;
A Te gra - to io m'in - chi - no:
U - ra, li - ber Svi - zzer, u - ra!
U - ra, li - ber Svi - zzer, u - ra!

Eu - re from - me See - le ahnt, Eu - re from - me See - le ahnt
Au ciel mon - tent plus joy - eux, Au ciel mon - tent plus joy - eux,
Li - ber - tà, con - cor - dia, a - mor, Li - ber - tà, con - cor - dia, a - mor
Ti has lu in sen - ti - ment, Ti has lu in sen - ti - ment
Ti - a or - ma sain - ta ferm, Ti - a or - ma sain - ta ferm,

Gott im heh - ren Va - ter - land,____
Les ac - cents d'un cœur pi - eux,____
All' El - ve - zia serba o - gnor,____
De tiu Bab sul fir - ma - ment,____
Dieu in tschêl, il Bap e - tern!____

Gott, im heh - ren, teu - ren Va - ter - land!
Les ac - cents é - mus d'un cœur____ pi - eux.
All' El - ve - zia ser - - - - - ba o - gnor.
De tiu Bab, tiu Bab, sul fir - - - ma - ment.
Dieu in tschêl, il Bap, il Bap____ e - tern!

GERMAN

2. *Kommst im Abendglüh'n daher,*
Find'ich dich im Sternenheer,
Dich, du Menschenfreundlicher, Liebender!
In des Himmels lichten Räumen
Kann ich froh und selig träumen!
Denn die fromme Seele ahnt } (twice)
Gott im hehren Vaterland!
Gott, im hehren, teuren Vaterland!

3. *Ziehst im Nebelflor daher,*
Such' ich dich im Wolkenmeer,
Dich, du Unergründlicher, Ewiger!
Aus dem grauen Luftgebilde
Tritt die Sonne klar und milde,
Und die fromme Seele ahnt } (twice)
Gott im hehren Vaterland!
Gott, im hehren, teuren Vaterland!

4. *Fährst im wilden Sturm daher,*
Bist du selbst uns Hort und Wehr,
Du, allmächtig Waltender, Rettender!
In Gewitternacht und Grauen
Lasst uns kindlich ihm vertrauen!
Ja, die fromme Seele ahnt } (twice)
Gott im hehren Vaterland!
Gott, im hehren, teuren Vaterland!

FRENCH

2. *Lorsqu'un doux rayon du soir*
   Joue encore dans le bois noir,
   Le cœur se sent plus heureux près de Dieu.
   Loin des vains bruits de la plaine
   L'âme en paix est plus sereine;
   Au ciel montent plus joyeux } (twice)
   Les accents d'un cœur pieux,
   Les accents émus d'un cœur pieux.

3. *Lorsque dans la sombre nuit*
   La foudre éclate avec bruit,
   Notre cœur pressent encore le Dieu fort.
   Dans l'orage et la détresse,
   Il est notre forteresse.
   Offrons-Lui des cœurs pieux, } (twice)
   Dieu nous bénira des cieux,
   Dieu nous bénira du haut des cieux.

4. *Des grands monts vient le secours,*
   Suisse! espère en Dieu toujours!
   Garde la foi des aïeux, vis comme eux!
   Sur l'autel de la partrie
   Mets tes biens, ton cœur, ta vie!
   C'est le trésor précieux } (twice)
   Que Dieu bénira des cieux,
   Que Dieu bénira du haut des cieux.

ITALIAN

2. *Se di stelle è un giubilo*
   La celeste sfera,
   Te ritrovo a sera,
   Ô Signor!
   Nella notte silenziosa
   L'alma mia in Te riposa:
   Libertà, concordia, amor, } (twice)
   All' Elvezia serba ognor!
   All' Elvezia serba ognor!

3. *Quando tristi velano*
   Atre nubi il cielo,
   Te presente anelo,
   Ô Signor!
   Se m'ascondi la Tua luce,
   Il mio spirito a Te m'adduce:
   Libertà, concordia, amor, } (twice)
   All' Elvezia serba ognor!
   All' Elvezia serba ognor!

4. *Quando rugge e strepita*
   Impetuoso il nembo,
   M'è ostel Tuo grembo,
   Ô Signor!
   In Te fido, Onnipossente;
   Deh, proteggi nostra gente:
   Libertà, concordia, amor, } (twice)
   All' Elvezia serba ognor,
   All' Elvezia serba ognor!

SURSELVISH*

2. *Cu il serendent sulegl*
   Resplendescha da smarvegl,
   Anflel Tei, miu Creatur,
   Amatur!
   Vesel nundumbreivlas steilas,
   Tarlischontas sco candeilas.
   Jeu hai lu in sentiment } (twice)
   De miu Bab sul firmament,
   De miu Bab, miu Bab sul firmament.

3. *Cu orcans sut il sulegl*
   Mettan tut en discavegl,
   Stai cun mei, o Directur,
   Salvatur!
   Els orcans ils pli sgarscheivels,
   Su cun Tiu agid statteivels,
   Jeu hai lu in sentiment } (twice)
   De miu Bab sul firmament,
   De miu Bab, miu Bab sul firmament.

*Rhaeto-Romansh of the Rhine valleys.

LADINISH*

2. *Eir la saira in splendur*
   Da las stailas in l'azur
   Tai chattain nus, creatur,
   Tuotpussant!
   Cur cha 'l firmamaint sclarescha
   In noss cours fidanza crescha.
   Tia orma sainta ferm,   } (twice)
   Dieu in tschêl, il Bap etern!
   Dieu in tschêl, il Bap, il Bap etern!

3. *Tü a nus nun est zoppà*
   Cur il tschêl in nüvlas sta,
   Tü imperscrutabel spiert,
   Tuotpussant!
   Tschêl e terra t'obedeschan,
   Vents e nüvlas secundeschan.
   Tia orma sainta ferm,   } (twice)
   Dieu in tschêl, il Bap etern!
   Dieu in tschêl, il Bap, il Bap etern!

4. *Eir l'orcan plü furius*
   Nun at muossa main a nus,
   Sco il dirigent dal muond,
   Tuotpussant!
   Eir in temporals terribels
   Sun teis uordens bain visibels.
   Tia orma sainta ferm,   } (twice)
   Dieu in tschêl, il Bap etern!
   Dieu in tschêl, il Bap, il Bap etern!

*Rhaeto-Romansh of Engadine.

ENGLISH

1. When the morning skies grow red
   And o'er us their radiance shed,
   Thou, O Lord, appeareth in their light.
   When the Alps glow bright with splendour,
   Pray to God, to Him surrender,
   For you feel and understand,   } (twice)
   That He dwelleth in this land.   } (twice)

2. In the sunset Thou art nigh
   And beyond the starry sky,
   Thou, O loving Father, ever near.
   When to Heaven we are departing,
   Joy and bliss Thou'lt be imparting,
   For we feel and understand   } (twice)
   That Thou dwellest in this land. } (twice)

3. When dark clouds enshroud the hills
   And grey mist the valley fills,
   Yet Thou art not hidden from Thy sons.
   Pierce the gloom in which we cower
   With Thy sunshine's cleansing power;
   Then we'll feel and understand   } (twice)
   That God dwelleth in this land.   } (twice)

SYRIA

Words by
KHALIL MARDAM BEY (1895 - 1959)

Music by
MOHAMMAD SALIM FLAYFEL (1899 - 1986)
and AHMAD SALIM FLAYFEL (1906 - 1991)

Ḥu - māt ad - di - yā - ri - 'a - lai - kum sal - ām

a - bat an tu - dal - la n - nu - fū - su - l - ki - rām 'a - rī - nu l - 'u - rū - ba - ti

bai - tun__ ḥa - rām wa - 'ar - ṣu š - ṣu - mū - si hi - man lā yu - ḍām

Officially adopted in 1936.

sa - mā - 'un la'am - ri - ka   au   ka - s-sa - mā'

Translation

Defenders of the realm,
Peace on you;
Our proud spirits will
Not be subdued.
The abode of Arabism,
A hallowed sanctuary;
The seat of the stars,
An inviolable preserve.

Syria's plains are
Towers in the heights,
Resembling the sky
Above the clouds.
A land resplendent
With brilliant suns,
Becoming another sky,
Or almost a sky.

TAIWAN

Words based on a speech by
SUN YAT-SEN (1866 - 1925)

Music by
CHENG MAO-YUN (1900 - 1957)
Arr. by HUANG CHIH and W. L. REED

Adopted in 1949.
* The words 'San Min Chu I' express Sun Yat-Sen's political philosophy of the Three People's Principles,
i.e. Government of the people, by the people, and for the people.

Translation by Tu T'ing-Hsiu

'San min chu I,' our aim shall be,
To found a free land, world peace be our stand.
Lead on comrades, vanguards ye are,
Hold fast your aim, by sun and star,
Be earnest and brave, your country to save,
One heart, one soul, one mind, one goal!

TAJIKISTAN

Words by
GULNAZAR KELDI (*b.* 1945)

Music by
SULAIMON YUDAKOV (1916 - 1990)
Arr. by W. L. REED

Officially adopted on 7 September, 1994.

1. *Diyori arjmandi mo,*
   Ba bakhti mo sari azizi tu baland bod,
   Saodati tu, davlati tu begazand bod.
   Zi durii zamonaho rasidayem,
   Ba zeri parchami tu saf kashidaem, kashidaem.

   CHORUS
   Zinda bosh, ey Vatan,
   Tojikistoni ozodi man!

2. *Baroi nangu nomi mo*
   Tu az umedi raftagoni mo nishonai,
   Tu bahri vorison jahoni jovidonai,
   Khazon namerasad ba navbahori tu,
   Ki mazrai vafo buvad kanori tu, kanori tu.

   CHORUS

3. *Tu modari yagonai,*
   Baqoi tu buvad baqoi khonadoni mo,
   Maromi tu buvad maromi jismu joni mo,
   Zi tu saodati abad nasibi most,
   Tu hastivu hama jahon habibi most, habibi most.

   CHORUS

Translation

1. Our rich region,
   For our happiness we want you to be always proud of us,
   Your happiness, your wealth let be always endless.
   We walked a lot to reach this time under your wing.

   CHORUS
   Long live our Homeland,
   Our free Tajikistan!

2. For our honour and conscience
   You are hope and memory of our ancestors that abandoned us,
   For our new generation you are eternal world,
   Your spring will never see fallen leaves,
   Let hope always accompany you, accompany you.

   CHORUS

3. You are mother that united us,
   Your prosperity is prosperity of our homes,
   Your health is a health of our body and soul,
   With you everlasting happiness accompanies us, accompanies us.

   CHORUS

TANZANIA

Words written collectively

Music by
ENOCH MANKAYI SONTONGA (1860 - 1904)
Arr. by V. E. WEBSTER

Adopted when Tanganyika achieved independence on 9 December, 1961 and retained when Tanzania was formed by the union of Tanganyika and Zanzibar on 26 April, 1964. The music is a shorter version of Nkosi Sikelel' iAfrika (see the National Anthems of South Africa and Zambia).

CHORUS

I - ba - ri - ki A - fri - ka I - ba - ri - ki A - fri - ka

Tu - ba - ri - ki wa - to - to wa A - fri - ka.

2. *Mungu ibariki Tanzania*
   Dumisha uhuru na Umoja
   Wake kwa Waume na Watoto
   Mungu Ibariki
   Tanzania na watu wake.

   CHORUS
   Ibariki Tanzania
   Ibariki Tanzania
   Tubariki watoto wa Tanzania.

Translation

1. God Bless Africa.
   Bless its leaders.
   Let Wisdom, Unity and Peace
   Be the shield of Africa and its people.

   CHORUS
   Bless Africa,
   Bless Africa,
   Bless the children of Africa.

2. God Bless Tanzania.
   Grant eternal Freedom and Unity
   To its sons and daughters.
   God Bless Tanzania and its people.

   CHORUS
   Bless Tanzania,
   Bless Tanzania,
   Bless the children of Tanzania.

THAILAND

Words by
LUANG SARANUPRAPAN (1896 - 1954)

Music by
PHRA CHEN-DURIYANG (1883 - 1968)

Pra thet___ thai ru - am nu ' a chat chu'a thai___ Pen pra

cha - rat___ pha thai kho'ng thai thuk suan Yu dam rong khong wai___ dai thang

muan Duay thai lu - an mai___ rak sa mak khi Thai ni

Adopted on 10 December, 1939.
Thailand also has a Royal Anthem (adopted in 1872) with words by Prince Narisara Nuvadtivongs (1863 - 1947) modified c.1913 by King Vajiravudh (1881 - 1925) and music by Pyotr Schurovsky (1850-1908).

Translation

Thailand embraces in its bosom all people of Thai blood.
Every inch of Thailand belongs to the Thais.
It has long maintained its sovereignty,
Because the Thais have always been united.
The Thai people are peace-loving,
But they are no cowards at war.
They shall allow no one to rob them of their independence,
Nor shall they suffer tyranny.
All Thais are ready to give up every drop of blood
For the nation's safety, freedom and progress.

TIMOR-LESTE

Words by
FRANSISCO BORJA DA COSTA (*b.* 1946)

Music by
AFONSO DE ARAÚJO (1947 - 1979) *
Arr. by MARTIN WEHN

Adopted unofficially in 1975 and officially in 2002.

* Composer disappeared in 1979.

<table>
<tr><td>

Pátria, Pátria, Timor-Leste, nossa Nação,
Glória aos heróis da nossa libertação.
Vencemos o colonialismo, gritamos:
Abaixo o imperialismo.

Terra livre, não, não, não à exploração.
Avante unidos firmes e decididos.
Na luta contra o imperialismo o, inimigo dos povos.
Até à vitória final, pelo caminho da revolução.

</td><td>

Translation

Fatherland, fatherland, East Timor our nation,
Glory to the heroes of our liberation
We defeat colonialism, we cry:
Down with imperialism.

Free land, no, no, no to exploitation.
Forward united firm and decided.
In the struggle against imperialism,
    the enemy of the people.
Until final victory, on the way to revolution.

</td></tr>
</table>

TOGO

Words and music by
ALEX CASIMIR-DOSSEH (*b.* 1923)
Arr. by ? HASSELMANN* and W. L. REED

1. *Sa - lut à toi, pa - ys de nos___ a - ïeux! Toi qui les ren - dais forts, pai - si - bles et joy - eux, Cul - ti - vant ver - tu, vail - lan - ce___ ___ Pour la pos - té - ri - té. Que vien - nent les ty - rans, ton cœur sou - pi - re*

Chosen as a result of a competition between Togolese composers. Originally adopted in 1960, it was replaced in 1979, restored in April, 1991 and reconfirmed by the Constitution on 14 October, 1992.

* First name unknown.

2. *Dans l'unité nous voulons te servir,*
   C'est bien là de nos cœurs le plus ardent désir
   Clamons fort notre devise
   Que rien ne peut ternir.
   Seuls artisans de ton bonheur ainsi que de ton avenir,
   Brisons partout les chaînes, la traîtrise
   Et nous te jurons toujours fidélité
   Et aimer, servir, se dépasser,
   Faire encore de toi sans nous lasser
   Togo Chéri, l'Or de l'Humanité.

Translation

1. Hail to thee, land of our forefathers,
   Thou who made them strong, peaceful and happy,
   Men who for posterity cultivated virtue and bravery.
   Even if tyrants shall come, thy heart yearns towards freedom.
   Togo arise! Let us struggle without faltering.
   Victory or death, but with dignity.
   God almighty, Thou alone hast made Togo prosper.
   People of Togo arise! Let us build the nation.

2. To serve thee in unity is the most burning desire of our hearts.
   Let us shout aloud our motto
   That nothing can tarnish.
   We the only builders of thy happiness and of thy future,
   Everywhere let us break chains and treachery,
   And we swear to thee for ever faith, love, service, untiring zeal,
   To make thee yet, beloved Togo, a golden example for humanity.

TONGA

Words by
PRINCE UELINGATONI NGU TUPOUMALOHI (1854 - 1885)

Music by
KARL GUSTAVUS SCHMITT (1834 - 1900)
Arr. by W. L. REED

The first reported singing of this National Anthem dates from 1874, but it was probably in use earlier.

'e mau lo tu, 'A ia 'o ku mau fai ni,
though un seen We know that Thou hast blessed our land;

Mo Ke ta li ho mau lo to, 'O ma la 'i 'a Tu pou.
Grant our earn est sup pli ca tion, Guard and save Tu pou our King.

TRINIDAD ᴀɴᴅ TOBAGO

Words and music by
PATRICK STANISLAUS CASTAGNE (1916-2000)

It was chosen as the result of a competition held by the Government, and adopted on 31 August, 1962.

TUNISIA

Words by
MUSTAFA SADIK AL-RAFII (1880 - 1937)
and ABDOUL KACEM CHABBI (1909 - 1934)

Music by
MOHAMAD ABDEL WAHAB (1915 - 1991) *
Arr. by W. L. REED

Adopted in 1987, replacing the former National Anthem.
* Mohamad Abdel Wahab also composed the music of the National Anthem of the United Arab Emirates.

Translation by M. A. S. Abdul Haleem

1. *Ḥumāta 'L-ḥimā Yā Ḥumāta 'L-ḥimā*
   Halummū, Halummū, Li-majdi 'Z-zaman
   Laqad Ṣarakhat Fil-'uruqi 'D-dimā
   Namūtu, Namūtu, Wa-yaḥya 'L-waṭan
   Li-tadwi 'S-samāwātu Bira 'dihā
   Li-tarmi 'Ṣ-ṣawā'iqu Nīrānahā
   Ilā 'Izzi Tūnis Ilā Majdihā
   Rijāla 'L-bilādi Wa-shubbānahā
   Falā 'Āsha Fī Tūnisa Man Khānahā
   Wa-lā 'Āsha Man Laysa Min Jundihā
   Namūtu Wa-naḥya 'Alā 'Ahdihā
   Ḥayata 'L-kirami Wa-mawta 'L- 'iẓām.

2. *Bilādi 'Ḥkumī wa' Mlikī Wa' Ṣ'adi*
   Falā 'Āsha Man Lam Ya'ish Sayyidā.
   Biḥurri Dami Wa-bimā Fī Yadī
   Anā Libilādī Wa-sha'bī Fidā.
   Laki 'L-majdu, Tūnusa, Fa'stamjidī
   Bi'izzati sha'biki Tūla 'L-madā,
   Wa-naḥnu usūdu 'L-waghā Fa'shhadī
   Wuthūba Usūdiki Yawma 'Ṣ-ṣdidam.

   Warithna 'S-sawā'ida Bayna 'L-umam
   Ṣukhūran, Ṣukhūran, Kaḥādhal 'L'binā
   Sawā'ida Yahtazzu Fawqaha 'L-'alam
   Nubāhī Kihi Wa-yubāhi Bīnā.
   Wa-fīhā Kafā Li-l 'Ulā Wa'-himam
   Wa-fīhā Li-a'da' I Tūnis Niqam
   Wa-fīhā Li-man Sālamūna' S-salām.

   Idha 'Sh-sha'bu Yawman Arāda 'L-ḥayāh
   Falā Budda An Yastajība 'L-qadar
   Walā Budda Li 'Z-ẓulmi An Yanjalī
   Walā Budda Li 'L-qaydi An Yankasir.

O defenders of the Homeland!
Rally around to the glory of our time!
The blood surges in our veins,
We die for the sake of our land.
Let the heavens roar with thunder.
Let thunderbolts rain with fire.
Men and youth of Tunisia,
Rise up for her might and glory.
No place for traitors in Tunisia,
Only for those who defend her!
We live and die loyal to Tunisia,
A life of dignity and a death of glory.

Rule Tunisia! Be wealthy and happy!
Only masters deserve to live
For Tunis and her people.
I give life and wealth.
Glory be yours, Tunisia,
Have full glory
With your people's might forever.
In battles we are lions,
Witness the assault of your lions.

As a nation we inherited
Arms like granite towers.
Holding aloft our proud flag flying,
We boast of it, it boasts of us,
Arms that achieve ambitions and glory,
Sure to realise our hopes,
Inflict defeat on foes,
Offer peace to friends.
When the people will to live,
Destiny must surely respond.
Oppression shall then vanish.
Fetters are certain to break.

TURKEY
Istıklâl Marsi
(The March of Independence)

Words by
MEHMET AKIF ERSOY (1873 - 1936)

Music by
OSMAN ZEKİ ÜNGÖR (1880 - 1958)
Arr. by T. M. CARTLEDGE

The words were adopted in 1921. The music was changed in 1932.

2. Çatma kurban olayım cehreni ey nazlı hilâl
   Kahraman ırkima bir gül ne bu şiddet bu celâl
   Sana olmaz dökülen kanlarımız sonra helâl
   Hakkıdır hakka tapan milletimin istiklâl.

Translation by T. M. Cartledge

1. Fear not and be not dismayed, this crimson flag will never fade.
   It is the last hearth that is burning for my nation,
   And we know for sure that it will never fail.
   It is my nation's star, shining forever,
   It is my nation's star and it is mine.

2. Frown not, fair crescent, for I am ready to die for you.
   Smile now upon my heroic nation, leave this anger,
   Lest the blood shed for thee be unblessed.
   Freedom is my nation's right,
   Freedom for us who worship God and seek what is right.

TURKMENISTAN

Words written collectively

Music by
VELI MUKHATOV (1916 - 2005)
Arr. by W. L. REED

Adopted in 2000.

Translation

CHORUS
Turkmenbashyn guran beyikh binasy,
Berkarar devletim, zhigerim-zhanym,
Batlaryn tezhi sen, diller senasy,
Dunye dursun, sen dur, Turkmenbashym!

1. *Zharnym gyrban sana erkana yurdum,*
   Mert pederlen ruzhy bardyp kenulde.
   Bitarap, garashsyz topragyn nurdur,
   Baydagyn belentdir dunyen enukde.

   CHORUS

2. *Gavdashtsyr tireler, anabdyr idler,*
   Onay-akhyr birdir byziy genymyz.
   Kharasatlar atmaz, synamrmaz sadler
   Necsimler det geril gerer iganymyz

   CHORUS

3. *Arkmdyr by daglar, penamdyr duzler!*
   Ykbalym, namysym, togabym, Vatak!
   Sana shek ctirse, kep bolsyn gozler,
   Gechyishim, gelzhegim, donimym. Vatak!

CHORUS
The great creation of Turkmenbasy,
Native land, sovereign state,
Turkmenistan, light and song of soul,
Long live and prosper for ever and ever!

1. I am ready to give life for native hearth,
   The spirit of ancestors descendants are famous for,
   My land is sacred. My flag flies in the world
   A symbol of the great neutral country flies.

   CHORUS

2. My nation is united and is veins of tribes
   Ancestors' blood, undying flows,
   Storms and misfortunes of times are not dreadful for us,
   Let us increase fame and honour!

   CHORUS

3. Mountains, rivers and beauty of steppes,
   Love and destiny, revelation of mine,
   Let my eyes go blind for any cruel look at you,
   Motherland of ancestors and heirs of mine!

TUVALU

Words and music by
AFAESE MANOA (*b.* 1942)

Maestoso

1. "Tu - va - lu mo te A - tu - a" Ko te Fa - ka - vae si -
1. "Tu - va - lu for The Al - migh-ty" Are the words we hold most

li, Ko te a - lu fo - ki te - na, O te ma - nu - ia ka -
dear; For as peo - ple or as lead - ers Of Tu - va - lu we all

toa; Lo - to la - si o fai, Tou—— ma - lo sao - lo -
share In the know - ledge that God E - ver rules in heav'n a -

Officially adopted on 1 October, 1978.

2. *Tuku atu tau pulega*
   Ki te pule mai luga,
   Kilo tonu ki ou mua
   Me ko ia e tautai.
   "Pule tasi mo ia"
   Ki te se gata mai,
   Ko tena mana
   Ko tou malosi tena.
   Pati lima kae kalaga
   Ulufonu ki te tupu.
   "Tuvalu ko tu saoloto"
   Ki te se gata mai.

Translation by J. F. Wilson

2. Let us trust our lives henceforward
   To the King to whom we pray,
   With our eyes fixed firmly on Him,
   He is showing us the way.
   "May we reign with Him in glory"
   Be our song for evermore,
   For His almighty power
   Is our strength from shore to shore.
   Shout aloud in jubilation.
   To the King Whom we adore.
   "Tuvalu free and united"
   Be our song for evermore!

UGANDA
Pearl of Africa

Words and music by
GEORGE WILBERFORCE KAKOMA (*b.* 1923)

1. Oh Uganda! may God uphold thee, We lay our future in thy hand. United, free, For liberty Together we'll always stand.

2. Oh Uganda! the land of freedom,
   Our love and labour we give,
   And with neighbours all
   At our country's call
   In peace and friendship we'll live.

3. Oh Uganda! the land that feeds us
   By sun and fertile soil grown,
   For our own dear land
   We'll always stand,
   The Pearl of Africa's Crown.

Selected through a competition, and adopted on 9 October, 1962.

UKRAINE

Words by
PAVLO PLATONOVICH CHYUBYNSKY (1839 - 1884)

Music by
MYKHAILO VERBYTSKY (1815 - 1870)
Arr. by HENRY COLEMAN

Sche ne vmer - la U - kra-i - ni, ni sla - va, ni vo - lia,

Sche nam, brat - tya mo - lo-di - yi u - smikh - net - sia do - lia:

Performed as a choral work in 1864 in the Ukraine Theatre in Lvov.
The music was adopted in 1992. Modified words were adopted in 2003.

Du - shu ti - lo my po - lo - shym za na - shu so - bo - du

I po - ka zhem, scho my, brat - tya, ko - zats' - ko - ho ro - du.

Translation by Ihor W. Slabicky

Ukraine's glory hasn't perished, nor her freedom
Upon us, fellow compatriots, fate shall smile once more.
Our enemies will vanish, like dew in the morning sun,
And we too shall rule, brothers, in a free land of our own.

We'll lay down our souls and bodies to attain our freedom, ⎫
And we'll show that we, brothers, are of the Kazak nation. ⎬ (twice)

UNITED ARAB EMIRATES

Words by
AREF AL SHEIKH ABDULLAH AL HASSAN *

Music by
MOHAMAD ABDEL WAHAB (1915 - 1991) †
Arr. by W. L. REED

Music adopted in 1971. Words adopted in 1996.

* Dates not yet available.

† Mohamad Abdel Wahab also composed the music of the National Anthem of Tunisia.

Iishi biladi, aasha ttihadu maratina,
Iishti li-shaabin dinuhu l-iislamu hadyuhu l-qur'anu.
Hassantuki bi-smi l-lahi ya watanu
Biladi, biladi, biladi, biladi
Hamaki l-'ilahu shurura z-zamani
Aqsamna an nabni naamalu
Naamalu nakhlusu naamalu nakhlusu
Mahma iishna nakhlusu nakhlusu
Dama l-aman wa-aasha l-aalamu ya imarati,
Ramzu l-uurubati:
Kulluna nafdiki bi-d-dima nurwiki
Nafdiki bi-l-'arwahi ya-watanu.

Translation

Live my country, the unity of our Emirates lives
You have lived for a nation
Whose religion is Islam and guide is the Quran
I made you stronger in God's name oh homeland
My country, my country, my country, my country
God has protected you from the evils of the time
We have sworn to build and work
Work sincerely, work sincerely
As long as we live, we'll be sincere
The safety has lasted and the flag has lived oh our Emirates
The symbol of Arabism
We all sacrifice for you, we supply you with our blood
We sacrifice for you with our souls oh homeland.

UNITED KINGDOM
God Save The Queen

Author unknown*

Composer unknown†

* Earliest copy of the words in Gentleman's Magazine, 1745.
† The melody is the same as that of the National Anthem of Liechtenstein.
The National Anthem of the United Kingdom is also used in Anguilla, Bermuda, British Virgin Islands, Falkland Islands, Montserrat, Pitcairn Islands, St. Helena and Dependencies and Turks & Caicos Islands. The Cayman Islands have their own National Song.

Long to__ reign__ o - ver us: God__ save the Queen.

2. O Lord our God arise,
Scatter her enemies,
And make them fall:
Confound their politics,
Frustrate their knavish tricks,
On Thee our hopes we fix:
God save us all.

3. Thy choicest gifts in store
On her be pleased to pour;
Long may she reign:
May she defend our laws,
And ever give us cause
To sing with heart and voice:
God save the Queen.

UNITED STATES OF AMERICA
The Star-Spangled Banner

Words by
FRANCIS SCOTT KEY (1779 - 1843)

Composer unknown*

Words and music officially designated as the National Anthem by Act of Congress approved by the President, 3 March, 1931. The National Anthem of the United States of America is also used in American Samoa, Guam, Northern Mariana Islands, Puerto Rico and U.S. Virgin Islands. The United States of America also has fifty State Songs. (see STATE SONGS OF AMERICA – Edited by M.J. Bristow).

* The English composer John Stafford Smith (c. 1750-1836) in his fifth collection of glees (1799) published an arrangement of 'To Anacreon in Heaven', the tune to which Francis Scott Key later wrote 'The Star-Spangled Banner'. This has led to his being mistakenly regarded as the composer of the tune, whose actual origin is unknown.

land_____ of the free and the home of the brave?

2. On the shore, dimly seen through the mists of the deep,
   Where the foe's haughty host in dread silence reposes,
   What is that which the breeze, o'er the towering steep,
   As it fitfully blows, half conceals, half discloses?
   Now it catches the gleam of the morning's first beam,
   In full glory reflected now shines on the stream;
   'Tis the Star-Spangled Banner, O long may it wave
   O'er the land of the free and the home of the brave!

3. O thus be it ever when free man shall stand
   Between their loved homes and the war's desolation!
   Blest with victory and peace, may the heaven-rescued land
   Praise the Power that hath made and preserved us a nation.
   Then conquer we must, for our cause it is just,
   And this be our motto: 'In God is our trust.'
   And the Star-Spangled Banner in triumph shall wave
   O'er the land of the free and the home of the brave.

URUGUAY

Words by
FRANCISCO ESTEBAN ACUÑA DE FIGUEROA (1791 - 1862) *

Music by
FRANCISCO JOSÉ DEBALI (1791 - 1859) †

The words were adopted on 12 July, 1845 and the music was adopted on 25 July, 1848. There are eleven verses.
* Francisco de Figueroa also wrote the words for the National Anthem of Paraguay.
† Francisco José Debali also composed the music for the National Anthem of Paraguay.

rien - do tam - bién li - ber - tad! tam - bién li - ber -

tad! tam - bién li - ber - tad! ¡Li - ber -

tad o con glo - ria mo - rir! Es el vo - to que el al - ma pro -

nun - cia Y que he - ro - i - cos sa - bre - mos cum - plir Es el

Translation by T. M. Cartledge

CHORUS

Eastern landsmen, our country or the tomb! } (twice)
Freedom, or with glory to die!
This is the vow that our souls take
And which we know how, courageously, to fulfil, } (twice)
Know how to fulfil,
Know how to fulfil.   } (three times)

VERSE

Freedom, freedom, eastern landsmen,
This cry saved our country,
Inflaming its brave men   } (twice)
With enthusiasm in fierce battles.
We merited the glory of this sacred gift.
Let tyrants tremble!

CHORUS

Let tyrants tremble,
Let tyrants tremble!

VERSE

Ah, in the fight we shall clamour for freedom
And, dying, still cry for it.

CHORUS

In the fight we shall clamour for freedom
And, dying, still cry for it,
And, dying, still cry for it,
Still cry for it,
Still cry for it.

Eastern landsmen... (repeat first six lines). (with internal repeats)

UZBEKISTAN

Words by
ABDULLA ORIPOV (*b.* 1941)

Music by
MUTAL BURHONOV (1916 - 2002)
Arr. by W. L. REED

Adopted in 1992.

1. *Serquyāsh, hur olkam, elga bakht najāt*
   Sen ozing dostlarin yoldāsh, mehribān!
   Yashnagay ta abad ilmu fan, ijād,
   Shukhrating pārlasin tāki bār jahān!

   CHORUS
   Altin bu vādiylar - jān Ozbekistān,
   Ajdādlār mardāna ruhi senga yār!
   Ulugh khalq qudrati josh urgan zamān,
   Ālamni mahliyā aylagan diyār!

2. *Baghri keng ozbekning ochmas iymāni.*
   Erkin, yāsh avlādlar senga zor qanāt!
   Istiqlāl mash'ali, tinchlik pāsbāni,
   Khaqsevar āna yurt, mangu bol ābād!

   CHORUS

Translation

1. Stand tall, my free country, good fortune and salvation to you,
   You yourself a companion to friends, Oh! Loving one!
   Flourish, Oh! Creator of eternal knowledge and science,
   May your fame for ever shine bright!

   CHORUS
   These valleys are golden - my dear Uzbekistan,
   Our forefathers' manly spirits your companion!
   Strength of great people in turbulent times
   Made this land the world's joy!

2. Oh! Generous Uzbek, your faith will not fade,
   Free, young generations are your mighty wings!
   The torch of independence, guardians of peace,
   Oh! Worthy motherland, flourish and prosper eternally!

   CHORUS

VANUATU

Words and music by
FRANÇOIS VINCENT AYSSAV (*b.* 1955)

Adopted in 1980.

2. *Plante fasin blong bifo i stap,*
   Plante fasin blong tedei,
   Be yumi i olsem wan nomo,
   Hemia fasin blong yumi!

   CHORUS

3. *Yumi save plante wok i stap,*
   Long ol aelan blong yumi,
   God i help em yumi evriwan,
   Hemi papa blong yumi.

   CHORUS

Translation by Parai K. Tamei

CHORUS
We are happy to proclaim
We are the People of Vanuatu !

1. God has given us this land;
   This gives us great cause for rejoicing.
   We are strong, we are free in this land;
   We are all brothers.

   CHORUS

2. We have many traditions
   And we are finding new ways.
   Now we shall be one People,
   We shall be united for ever.

   CHORUS

3. We know there is much work to be done
   On all our islands.
   May God, our Father, help us!

   CHORUS

VATICAN CITY STATE
Inno e Marcia Pontificale
(Hymn and Pontifical March)

Latin words by
RAFFAELLO LAVAGNA (*b.* 1918)

Music by
CHARLES-FRANÇOIS GOUNOD (1818 - 1893)
Arr. by FABIO LAZZATI

This became the official hymn in 1950. It is played (1) In the presence of the Holy Father. (2) In the presence of one of his Special Legates. (3) On the occasion of presentation of Credential Letters by a Nuncio of the Holy See.

Marcia Pontificale (Pontifical March)

Tu es pa - cis vin - dex Tu es u - ni - ta - tis cu - stos

vi - gil li - be - ta - tis de - fen - sor in Te po - te -

Poco più lento

stas. O Ro - ma no - bi - lis Ro - ma fe - lix

ff

rallentatissimo

tu no - bi - lis.

Translation

HYMN

O happy Rome – O noble Rome:
You are the See of Peter, who in Rome shed his blood,
Peter who was given the keys of the kingdom of heaven.
Pontiff, You are the successor of Peter;
Pontiff, You are the master strengthening your brethren;
Pontiff, You the servant of the servants of God,
Fisher of men, you are the shepherd of the flock,
Binding heaven and earth.

PONTIFICAL MARCH

Pontiff, you are the vicar of Christ on earth,
Rock amidst the breakers, light in the darkness;
You are the avenger of peace, you are the guardian of unity,
Watchful defender of freedom; in you is the power.
Pontiff, You are the firm stone,
And on this stone is built the Church of God.
O happy Rome – O noble Rome.

VENEZUELA

Words by
VICENTE SALIAS (1786 - 1814)

Music by
JUAN JOSÉ LANDAETA (1780 - 1814)

Adopted on 25 May, 1881.

2. *Gritemos con brío:*
    Muera la opresión!
    Compatriotas fieles
    La fuerza es la unión:
    Y desde el Empíreo
    El Supremo Autor,
    Un sublime aliento
    Al pueblo infundió.

    CHORUS

3. *Unida con lazos*
    Que el cielo formó,
    La América toda
    Existe en Nación;
    Y si el despotismo
    Levanta la voz,
    Seguid el ejemplo
    Que Caracas dió.

    CHORUS

Translation by T. M. Cartledge

CHORUS
Glory to the brave nation
Which shook off the yoke,
Respecting law, virtue and honour. } (twice)

SOLO
"Off with the chains! Off with the chains!" (repeated phrase by CHORUS)
Cried the Lord, cried the Lord,   (repeated phrase by CHORUS)
And the poor man in his hovel
Implored freedom.
At this holy name, there trembled
The vile selfishness that had triumphed,
The vile selfishness that had triumphed.

CHORUS
Glory to the brave nation... etc. (repeat top 3 lines, with internal repeat)

2. Let's cry out aloud:
    Down with oppression!
    Faithful countrymen, your strength
    Lies in your unity;
    And from the heavens
    The supreme Creator
    Breathed a sublime spirit
    Into the nation.

    CHORUS

3. United by bonds
    Made by heaven,
    All America exists
    As a Nation;
    And if tyranny
    Raises its voice,
    Follow the example
    Given by Caracas.

    CHORUS

VIETNAM
Tien Quan Ca
(March to the Front)

Words and music by
NGUYEN VAN CAO (1923 - 1995)

Adopted in 1946. The re-unification of North Vietnam (Socialist Democratic People's Republic) and South Vietnam (Republic) took place in 1976. The National Anthem of North Vietnam was retained.

608

French Translation

1. *Soldats vietnamiens, nous allons de l 'avant,*
   Mus par une même volonté de sauver la patrie.
   Nos pas redoublés sonnent sur la route longue et rude.
   Notre drapeau, rouge du sang de la victoire, porte l 'âme de la nation.
   Le lointain grondement des canons rythme les accents de notre marche.
   Le chemin de la gloire se pave de cadavres ennemis.
   Triomphant des difficultés, ensemble, nous édifions nos bases de résistance.
   Jurons de lutter sans répit pour la cause du peuple.
   Courons vers le champ de bataille!
   En avant! Tous ensemble, en avant!
   Notre patrie vietnamienne est solide et durable.

2. *Soldats vietamiens, nous allons de l 'avant,*
   L 'etoile d'or au vent
   Conduisant notre peuple et notre patrie hors de la misère et des souffrances.
   Unissons nos efforts dans la lutte pour l 'édification de la vie nouvelle.
   Debout! d 'un même élan, rompons nos fers!
   Depuis si longtemps, nous avons contenu notre haine!
   Soyons prêts à tous les sacrifices et notre vie sera radieuse.
   Jurons de lutter sans répit pour la cause du peuple,
   Courons vers le champ de bataille!
   En avant! Tous ensemble, en avant!
   Notre patrie vietnamienne est solide et durable.

Translation

1. Soldiers of Vietnam, we go forward,
   With the one will to save our Fatherland,
   Our hurried steps are sounding on the long and arduous road.
   Our flag, red with the blood of victory, bears the spirit of our country.
   The distant rumbling of the guns mingles with our marching song.
   The path to glory passes over the bodies of our foes.
   Overcoming all hardships, together we build our resistance bases.
   Ceaselessly for the people's cause let us struggle,
   Let us hasten to the battle-field !
   Forward! All together advancing!
   Our Vietnam is strong, eternal.

2. Soldiers of Vietnam, we go forward!
   The gold star of our flag in the wind
   Leading our people, our native land, out of misery and suffering.
   Let us join our efforts in the fight for the building of a new life.
   Let us stand up and break our chains.
   For too long have we swallowed our hatred.
   Let us keep ready for all sacrifices and our life will be radiant.
   Ceaselessly for the people's cause let us struggle,
   Let us hasten to the battle-field!
   Forward! All together advancing!
   Our Vietnam is strong, eternal.

WALES
Hen Wlad fy Nhadau
(Land of my Fathers)

Words by
EVAN JAMES (1809 - 1893)
English versification by
W. S. GWYNN WILLIAMS

Music by
JAMES JAMES (1833 - 1902) *
Arr. by W. S. GWYNN WILLIAMS
and W. L. REED

1. Mae hen wlad fy nhad-au yn an nwyl i— mi, Gwlad beirdd a chan-tor-ion, en-wog-ion o fri; Ei gwr-ol ry - fel-wyr, gwlad-gar-wyr tra-

1. The land of my fath-ers is dear un-to— me, Old land where the min-strels are hon-oured and free; Its war-ring de - fen-ders so gal-lant and—

First sung at the famous Llangollen Eisteddfod of 1858, and now regarded as having the status of a National Anthem.
* It is also sung as an anthem in Brittany, to a Breton version by J. Taldir.
English versification by permission of the Gwyn Publishing Co. (Copyright 1950).

mâd,   Tros rydd - id coll - as - ant   eu   gwaed._____
brave,   For free - dom their   life's blood they   gave._____

f CHORUS

Gwlad,   gwlad,   pleid - iol   wyf_____   i'm
Home,   home,   true_____ am   I_____   to

gwlad,   Tra môr   yn_____ fur   i'r   bur   hoff_____
home,   While seas   se - cure   the   land   so_____

D. %

bau,   O   bydd - ed i'r   hen - iaith bar - hau.
pure,   O   may the   old   lan - guage en - dure.

2. *Hen Gymru fynyddig, paradwys y bardd,*
   Pob dyffryn, pob clogwyn i'm golwg sydd hardd;
   Trwy deimlad gwladgarol, mor swynol yw si
   Ei nentydd, afonydd, i mi.

   CHORUS

3. *Os treisiodd y gelyn fy ngwlad tan ei droed,*
   Mae hen iaith y Cymry mor fyw ag erioed;
   Ni luddiwyd yr awen gan erchyll law brad,
   Na thelyn berseiniol fy ngwlad.

   CHORUS

2. Old land of the mountains, the Eden of bards,
   Each gorge and each valley a loveliness guards;
   Through love of my country, charmed voices will be
   Its streams, and its rivers, to me.

   CHORUS

3. Though foemen have trampled my land 'neath their feet,
   The language of Cambria still knows no retreat;
   The muse is not vanquished by traitor's fell hand,
   Nor silenced the harp of my land.

   CHORUS

YEMEN

Words by
ABDULLAH ABDULWAHAB NOA'MAN (1916 - 1982)

Music by
AYYOAB TARISH ABSI (*b.* 1943)
Arr. by W. L. REED

Adopted on 22 May, 1990. The union of South Yemen (People's Republic) and North Yemen (Arab Republic) took place on 22 May, 1990. The National Anthem of South Yemen was retained.

Raddidī Ayyatuha 'D-dunyā Nashīdī
Raddidīhī Wa-a 'īdī Wa-a 'īdī
Wa 'Dhkurī Fī Farhatī Kulla Shahīdī
Wa'Mnahīhī Hullalan Min Daw'i 'Īdī
Raddidī Ayyatuha 'D-dunyā Nashīdī
'Ishtu Īmānī Wa-hubbī Umamiyyā
Wa-masīrī Fawqa Darbī 'Arabiyyā
Wa-sayabqā Nabdu Qalbī Yamaniyyā
Lan Tarā 'D-dunyā 'Alā Ardī Wasiyyā.

Translation by M. A. S. Abdul Haleem

Repeat, O World, my song.
Echo it over and over again.
Remember, through my joy, each martyr.
Clothe him with the shining mantles
Of our festival.
Repeat, O World, my song.
In faith and love I am part of mankind.
An Arab I am in all my life.
My heart beats in tune with Yemen.
No foreigner shall dominate over Yemen.

ZAMBIA

Words written collectively

Music by
ENOCH MANKAYI SONTONGA (1860 - 1904) *

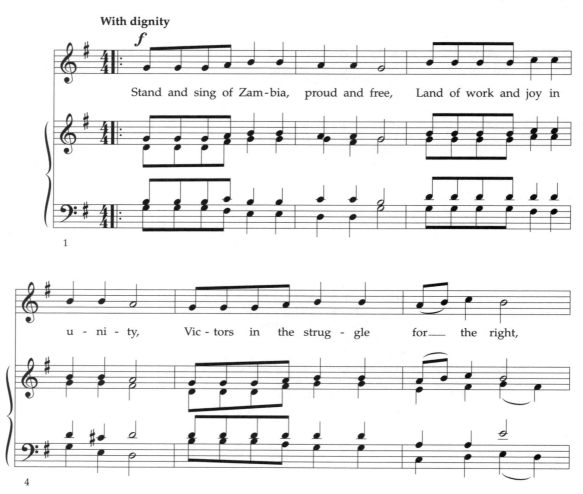

With dignity

Stand and sing of Zam-bia, proud and free, Land of work and joy in

u - ni - ty, Vic - tors in the strug - gle for the right,

*Originally written as a hymn tune at Lovedale Mission in Cape Province, South Africa.

The tune became well known throughout a large part of southern, central and eastern Africa, and the words were translated into many African languages. Indeed, it came to be popularly known as the Bantu National Anthem. The tune was officially adopted by Tanganyika (later Tanzania) as its National Anthem on the achievement of independence in 1961. New words have been specially written for Zambia. A competition was held and these words were produced as a composite version after a study of the ideas and the words of the six leading entries in the competition.

Officially adopted 24 October, 1964. It was also adopted as part of the National Anthem of South Africa in 1994.

praise— to thee! All one, strong— and free.———

19

2. One land and one nation is our cry,
   Dignity and peace 'neath Zambia's sky,
   Like our noble eagle in it's flight,
   Zambia, praise to thee,
   All one proud and free.

3. Africa is our mother land,
   Fashioned with and blessed by God's good hand,
   Let us all our people join as one,
   Zambia praise to thee,
   All one proud and free.

   CHORUS (after 3rd verse only)
   Praise be to God,
   Praise be, praise be, praise be,
   Bless our great nation,
   Zambia, Zambia, Zambia.
   Free men we stand
   Under the flag of our land.
   Zambia – praise to thee
   All one, strong and free.

1. *Lumbanyeni Zambia, no kwanga,*
   Ne cilumba twange tuumfwane,
   Mpalume sha bulwi bwa cine,
   Twaliilubula.
   Twikatane bonse.

2. *Bonse tuli bana ba Africa,*
   Uwasenaminwa na Lesa,
   Nomba bonse twendele pamo,
   Twaliilubula.
   Twikatane bonse.

3. *Fwe lukuta lwa Zambia lonse,*
   Twikatane tubyo mutende,
   Pamo nga lubambe mu mulu,
   Lumbanyeni Zambia.
   Twikatane bonse.

   CHORUS (after 3rd verse only)
   Lumbanyeni,
   Lesa, Lesa, wesu,
   Apale calo,
   Zambia, Zambia, Zambia.
   Fwe bantungwa
   Mu luunga lwa calo.
   Lumbanyeni Zambia.
   Twikatane bonse.

ZIMBABWE
Kalibusiswe Ilizwe leZimbabwe
Blessed be the Land of Zimbabwe

Words by
SOLOMON MUTSWAIRO (*b.* 1924)

Music by
FRED LECTURE CHANGUNDEGA (*b.* 1954)
Arr. by W. L. REED

Officially adopted on 18 April, 1994.

(Ndebele)

2. *Khangelan' i Zimbabwe yon' ihlotshi si we*
   Ngezintaba lang' miful' e bu keka yo.
   I zulu kaline, izilimo zande;
   Iz' sebenzi zenam', abantu basuthe;
   Kalibusiswe ilizwe leZimbabwe.

3. *Nkosi bu sis' ilizwe le-thu leZimbabwe*
   Ilizwe labo khokho bethu thina sonke;
   Kusuk' eZambezi Kusiy' e Limpopo.
   Abakho kheli babe lobuqotho;
   Kalibusiswe ilizwe leZimbabwe.

(Shona)

2. *Tarisai Zimbabwe nyika yakashonge dzwa*
   Namakomo, nehova, zvinoyeve dza;
   Mvura ngainaye, minda ipe mbesa
   Vashandi vatuswe, ruzhinji rugutswe;
   Ngaikomborerwe nyika yeZimbabwe.

3. *Mwari ropafadzai nyika yeZimbabwe*
   Nyika yamadzitate guru edu to se;
   Kubva Zambezi Kusvika Limpopo,
   Navatungamiri vave nenduramo;
   Ngaikomborerwe nyika yeZimbabwe.

(English)

2. O lovely Zimbabwe, so wondrously adorned
   With mountains and rivers cascading, flowing free;
   May rain abound, and fertile fields.
   May we be fed, our labour blessed;
   And may the Almighty protect and bless our land.

3. O God, we beseech Thee to bless our native land;
   The land of our fathers bestowed upon us all;
   From Zambezi to Limpopo.
   May leaders be exemplary;
   And may the Almighty protect and bless our land.

EUROPEAN UNION

Music by
LUDWIG van BEETHOVEN (1770 - 1827) *
Arr. by W. L. REED

* The Anthem is the Prelude to 'Ode to Joy' from the fourth movement of the Ninth Symphony by Ludwig van Beethoven, chosen as the European Anthem by the Council of Europe in 1971-1972. There are words in German, but they are not sung at European Community events.

NATIONAL DAYS

AFGHANISTAN	27 April	Revolution Day, 1978
ALBANIA	11 January	National Day, 1946
	28 November	Independence Day, 1912
ALGERIA	1 November	Revolution Day, 1954
ANDORRA	8 September	Jungfrau von Meritxell Day, 1278
ANGOLA	11 November	Independence Day, 1975
ANTIGUA and BARBUDA	1 November	Independence Day, 1981
ARGENTINA	25 May	Revolution Day, 1810
	9 July	Independence Day, 1816
ARMENIA	23 September	Independence Day, 1991
AUSTRALIA	26 January	Australia Day, 1788
AUSTRIA	26 October	Flag Day, 1955
AZERBAIJAN	28 May	Independence Day, 1918
BAHAMAS, THE	10 July	Independence Day, 1973
BAHRAIN	16 December	Independence Day, 1961
BANGLADESH	21 February	Language Martyrs Day, 1952
	26 March	Independence Day, 1971
	16 December	Constitution Day, 1971
BARBADOS	30 November	Independence Day, 1966
BELARUS	27 July	Independence Day, 1990
BELGIUM	6 June	Birthday of H.M. King Albert II, 1934
	21 July	Independence Day, 1831
BELIZE	21 September	Independence Day, 1981
BÉNIN	1 August	Independence Day, 1960
BHUTAN	11 November	Birthday of H.M. King Jigme Singye Wangchuck, 1955
	17 December	National Day, 1907
BOLIVIA	6 August	Independence Day, 1825
BOSNIA and HERZEGOVINA	6 April	Independence Day, 1992
BOTSWANA	30 September	Independence Day, 1966
BRAZIL	7 September	Independence Day 1822
	15 November	Republic Day, 1889
BRUNEI DARUSSALAM	23 February	Independence Day, 1984
BULGARIA	3 March	National Day, 1878
BURKINA FASO	5 August	Independence Day, 1960
BURUNDI	1 July	Independence Day, 1962
CAMBODIA	31 October	Birthday of H.M. King Norodom Sihanouk, 1922
	9 November	Independence Day, 1953
CAMEROON	20 May	Constitution Day, 1972
CANADA	1 July	Canada Day, 1867
CAPE VERDE	5 July	Independence Day, 1975
CENTRAL AFRICAN REPUBLIC	1 December	National Day, 1958
CHAD	11 August	Independence Day, 1960
CHILE	18 September	Independence Day, 1818
CHINA	1 October	Founding of People's Republic, 1949
COLOMBIA	20 July	Independence Day, 1810
COMOROS, THE	6 July	Independence Day, 1975
CONGO (Democratic Republic)	30 June	Independence Day, 1960
	24 November	National Day, 1965
CONGO (Republic)	15 August	Independence Day, 1960
COSTA RICA	15 September	Independence Day, 1821
CROATIA	30 May	Independence Day, 1991
CUBA	1 January	Liberation Day, 1959
CYPRUS	1 October	National Day, 1963
CZECH REPUBLIC	28 October	Founding of the Republic, 1918

DENMARK	16 April	Birthday of H.M. Queen Margrethe II, 1940
	5 June	Constitution Day, 1953
DJIBOUTI	27 June	Independence Day, 1977
DOMINICA	3 November	Independence Day, 1978
DOMINICAN REPUBLIC	27 February	Independence Day, 1844
ECUADOR	10 August	Independence Day, 1809
EGYPT	18 June	Evacuation Day, 1956
	23 July	Revolution Day, 1952
	6 October	Armed Forces Day, 1973
EL SALVADOR	15 September	Independence Day, 1821
ENGLAND	23 April	Saint George's Day, 1415
EQUATORIAL GUINEA	12 October	Independence Day, 1968
ERITREA	24 May	Independence Day, 1993
ESTONIA	24 February	National Day, 1918
ETHIOPIA	28 May	Victory Day, 1991
FIJI	10 October	Independence Day, 1970
FINLAND	6 December	Independence Day, 1917
FRANCE	14 July	Bastille Day, 1789
GABON	17 August	Independence Day, 1960
GAMBIA, THE	18 February	Independence Day, 1965
	24 April	Republic Day, 1970
GEORGIA	26 May	Independence Day, 1918
GERMANY	3 October	Day of Unity, 1990
GHANA	6 March	Independence Day, 1957
GIBRALTAR	10 September	National Day, 1993
GREECE	25 March	Independence Day, 1821
GRENADA	7 February	Independence Day, 1974
GUATEMALA	15 September	Independence Day, 1821
GUINEA	2 October	Republic Day, 1958
GUINEA-BISSAU	24 September	Independence Day, 1974
GUYANA	23 February	Republic Day, 1970
HAITI	1 January	Independence Day, 1804
HONDURAS	15 September	Independence Day, 1821
HUNGARY	15 March	National Day, 1991
	20 August	Saint Stephen's Day, 1990
	23 October	Anniversary of the Revolution, 1956 and Proclamation of the Hungarian Republic, 1989
ICELAND	17 June	Anniversary of Establishment of the Republic, 1944
INDIA	26 January	Republic Day, 1950
	15 August	Independence Day, 1947
INDONESIA	17 August	Independence Day, 1945
IRAN	11 February	Revolution Day, 1979
	1 April	Proclamation of Islamic Republic, 1979
IRAQ	17 July	National Day, 1968
IRISH REPUBLIC	17 March	Saint Patrick's Day, 1681
ISLE OF MAN	5 July	National Day, 1752
ISRAEL	14 May	Independence Day, 1948
ITALY	2 June	Anniversary of Proclamation of the Republic, 1946
IVORY COAST	7 August	Independence Day, 1960

JAMAICA	6 August	Independence Day, 1962
	(This is celebrated the First Monday of August each year)	
JAPAN	11 February	Founding of Imperial Dynasty, 660BC
	3 May	Constitution Day, 1947
	23 December	Birthday of H.M. Emperor Akihito, 1933
JORDAN	30 January	Birthday of H.M. King Abdulla, 1962
	25 May	Independence Day, 1946
KAZAKHSTAN	16 December	Independence Day, 1991
KENYA	12 December	Independence Day, 1963 and Republic Day, 1964
	20 October	Kenyatta Day, 1978
KIRIBATI	12 July	Independence Day, 1979
KOREA (North)	8 September	Constitution Day, 1948
KOREA (South)	15 August	Independence Day, 1948
KUWAIT	25 February	National Day, 1961
KYRGYZSTAN	31 August	Independence Day, 1991
LAOS	2 December	Proclamation of People's Democratic Republic, 1975
LATVIA	18 November	National Day, 1918
LEBANON	22 November	Independence Day, 1943
LESOTHO	17 July	Birthday of H.M. King Letsie III, 1963
	4 October	Independence Day, 1966
LIBERIA	26 July	Independence Day, 1847
LIBYA	1 September	Revolution Day, 1969
LIECHTENSTEIN	14 February	Birthday of H.S.H. Prince Hans Adam II, 1945
	15 August	National Day, 1940
LITHUANIA	16 February	Independence Day, 1918
LUXEMBOURG	16 April	Birthday of H.R.H. Grand Duke Henri, 1955
	23 June	National Day, 1962
MACEDONIA	8 September	Independence Day, 1991
MADAGASCAR	26 June	Independence Day, 1960
MALAWI	6 July	Independence Day, 1964 and Republic Day, 1966
MALAYSIA	31 August	Independence Day, 1957
MALDIVES, THE	26 July	Independence Day, 1965
MALI	22 September	Republic Day, 1960
MALTA	21 September	Independence Day, 1964
MARSHALL ISLANDS	21 October	Compact Day, 1986
MAURITANIA	28 November	Independence Day, 1960
MAURITIUS	12 March	Independence Day, 1968
MEXICO	16 September	Independence Day, 1810
MICRONESIA	10 May	Constitution Day, 1979
	3 November	Independence Day, 1986
MOLDOVA	27 August	Independence Day, 1991
MONACO	14 March	Birthday of H.S.H. Prince Albert II, 1958
	19 November	Saint Rainier Day, 1949
MONGOLIA	11 July	Independence Day, 1921
	26 November	Republic Day, 1924
MOROCCO	23 July	Anniversary of the Throne, 1999
	21 August	Birthday of H.M. King Mohamed VI, 1963
	18 November	Independence Day, 1956
MOZAMBIQUE	25 June	Independence Day, 1975
MYANMAR	4 January	Independence Day, 1948
NAMIBIA	21 March	Independence Day, 1990
NAURU	31 January	Independence Day, 1968

NEPAL	11 January	Unity Day, 1775
	7 July	Birthday of H.M. King Gyanendra, 1947
	9 November	Constitution Day, 1990
NETHERLANDS	31 January	Birthday of H.M. Queen Beatrix, 1938
	5 May	Liberation Day, 1945
NEW ZEALAND	6 February	Waitangi Day, 1840
NICARAGUA	15 September	Independence Day, 1821
NIGER	3 August	Independence Day, 1960
	18 December	Republic Day, 1958
NIGERIA	1 October	Independence Day, 1960
NORWAY	21 February	Birthday of H.M. King Harald V, 1937
	17 May	Constitution Day, 1814
OMAN	18 November	Birthday of H.M. The Sultan Qaboos Bin-Said, 1940
PAKISTAN	23 March	Republic Day, 1956
	14 August	Independence Day, 1947
PALAU	9 July	Constitution Day, 1979
	1 October	Independence Day, 1994
PANAMA	3 November	Independence Day, 1903
PAPUA NEW GUINEA	16 September	Independence Day, 1975
PARAGUAY	15 May	Independence Day, 1811
PERU	28 July	Independence Day, 1821
PHILIPPINES, THE	12 June	Independence Day, 1898
POLAND	3 May	Constitution Day, 1791
PORTUGAL	25 April	Freedom Day, 1974
	10 June	National Day, 1580
	5 October	Republic Day, 1910
	1 December	Restoration Day, 1640
QATAR	3 September	Independence Day, 1971
ROMANIA	1 December	National Day, 1990
RUSSIAN FEDERATION	26 December	National Day, 1991
RWANDA	1 July	Independence Day, 1962
SAINT KITTS and NEVIS	19 September	Independence Day, 1983
SAINT LUCIA	22 February	Independence Day, 1979
SAINT VINCENT and THE GRENADINES	27 October	Independence Day, 1979
SAMOA	5 January	Birthday of King Malietoa Tanumafili II, 1913
	1 June	National Day, 1962
SAN MARINO	3 September	Marinus Day, 301
SÃO TOMÉ and PRÍNCIPE	12 July	Independence Day, 1975
SAUDI ARABIA	23 September	National Day, 1964
SCOTLAND	30 November	Saint Andrew's Day, 832
SÉNÉGAL	4 April	Independence Day, 1960
SERBIA and MONTENEGRO	29 November	Republic Day, 1945
SEYCHELLES	5 June	Liberation Day, 1977
	29 June	Independence Day, 1976
SIERRA LEONE	27 April	Republic Day, 1961
SINGAPORE	9 August	Independence Day, 1965
SLOVAKIA	1 January	Independence Day, 1993
	5 July	St Cyril & Method's Day, 863
	29 August	National Uprising Day, 1944
	1 September	Constitution Day, 1992

SLOVENIA	25 June	Independence Day, 1991
SOLOMON ISLANDS	7 July	Independence Day, 1978
SOMALIA	1 July	Republic Day, 1960
SOUTH AFRICA	31 May	Republic Day, 1961
	16 June	Soweto Uprising, 1976
SPAIN	5 January	Birthday of H.M. King Juan Carlos I, 1938
	12 October	National Day, 1918
SRI LANKA	4 February	Independence Day, 1948
SUDAN	1 January	Independence Day, 1956
SURINAM	25 November	Independence Day, 1975
SWAZILAND	19 April	Birthday of H.M. King Mswati III, 1968
	6 September	Independence Day, 1968
SWEDEN	30 April	Birthday of H.M. King Carl XVI Gustaf, 1946
	6 June	Flag Day, 1523
SWITZERLAND	1 August	Anniversary of the Foundation of Confederation, 1291
SYRIA	8 March	Revolution Day, 1963
	17 April	Independence Day, 1946
TAIWAN	10 October	National Day, 1911
TAJIKISTAN	9 September	Independence Day, 1991
TANZANIA	26 April	Union Day, 1964
THAILAND	6 April	Chakri Day, 1782
	23 October	Chulalongkorn Day, 1910
	5 December	Birthday of H.M. King Bhumibol Adulyadej, 1927
	10 December	Constitution Day, 1932
TIMOR-LESTE	20 May	Independence Day, 2002
TOGO	13 January	National Liberation Day, 1963
TONGA	4 June	Independence Day, 1970
	4 July	Birthday of H.M. King Taufa'ahau Typou IV, 1918
TRINIDAD and TOBAGO	31 August	Independence Day, 1962
	24 September	Republic Day, 1976
TUNISIA	20 March	Independence Day, 1956
	25 July	Republic Day, 1957
	7 November	National Day, 1987
TURKEY	23 April	National Sovereign Day, 1920
	19 May	Atatuk Day, 1919
	30 August	Victory Day, 1922
	29 October	Republic Day, 1923
TURKMENISTAN	27 October	Independence Day, 1991
TUVALU	1 October	Independence Day, 1978
UGANDA	9 October	Independence Day, 1962
UKRAINE	28 June	Constitution Day, 1992
	24 August	Independence Day, 1991
UNITED ARAB EMIRATES	2 December	Federation Day, 1971
UNITED KINGDOM	21 April	Birthday of H.M. Queen Elizabeth II, 1926
UNITED STATES OF AMERICA	4 July	Independence Day, 1776
	27 November	Thanksgiving Day, 1621
		(This is celebrated the Fourth Thursday of November each year)
URUGUAY	25 August	Independence Day, 1825
UZBEKISTAN	31 August	Independence Day, 1991
VANUATU	30 July	Independence Day, 1980
VATICAN CITY STATE	16 April	Birthday of H.H. Pope Benedict XVI, 1927
VENEZUELA	5 July	Independence Day, 1830
VIETNAM	2 September	Independence Day, 1945

WALES	1 March	Saint David's Day, 1398
YEMEN	22 May	Republic Day, 1990
ZAMBIA	24 October	Independence Day, 1964
ZIMBABWE	18 April	Independence Day, 1980
EUROPEAN UNION	9 May	Europe Day, 1985
UNITED NATIONS	24 October	United Nations Day, 1945